A MODERN YOGI
A different kinda memoir

by Charu Puri

ISBN 978-0-9936946-1-5

Table of Contents

Reinventing myself

My birth name is Charu Puri. I was Charu up until age sixteen. Growing up in a predominantly white city and trying to get people to pronounce my name correctly was challenging most of the time. I got Charlie, Cheroo or Sheroo, like the mouse. Yup – shrew, like the mouse. Great, I've been downsized from a human being to a mouse. Finally, one day while I was sitting at my kitchen table late at night, when the rest of the house was fast asleep, I decided that was it. I was gonna change my name.

That was the obvious reason for wanting to change my name. But there was more to it than that. Already at sixteen, something within me knew that when I grew up, whatever it was that I'd be doing in my life, a lot of people would know me. I would have to meet a lot of people, and I wasn't sure that Charu Puri was gonna fly. So I got out a piece of lined paper, picked up a favourite pencil and went through the alphabet to see what letter I liked best for my new name. I finally got it narrowed down to R. I started sounding it out: Ru Ra Rai, going it over in my head, scribbling it down on paper. Did I want a one-syllable or a two-syllable name? So many things to think about. Another key letter for me was the Y. I thought to myself, "There are not a lot of names with a Y in them. And I could be really creative doing signatures with a name that had a Y in it.

So that was it. "Reyna" came to life that night on my lined school paper. From then on, whenever I met someone new in my life, I introduced myself as Reyna. At first, my existing circle of friends would turn their heads and say, "Who?" They got used to it fairly soon, though. They just assumed it was my middle name that I'd kept hidden for years. And some thought Charu was a pet name or something.

I'm back to Charu now. Well, I always was Charu. I just had a pseudonym that just stuck with me for years. By now, I think the world is smart enough that people can pronounce all kinds of letter combinations. I would hope so. I was sixteen at the time, and so was everyone else around me. That's the big chunk of a difference that I didn't recognize back then. At that age, it's all about being cool, etc. Hopefully, we're all a bit more world savvy now. Anyhow, a name is just a name. It's not your whole identity – it's only a part of it. So don't be confused if you see the name Reyna mentioned more often than Charu. I was still going by that name until very recently.

ACKNOWLEDGEMENTS

I would like to thank the following people for giving me their light for this book. My gratitude and blessings to all of you for your gifts of wisdom and knowledge.

I thank God Almighty. This book was written with the helping hand of God. It's how it got on paper.

I thank my dear brother and friend, Neil Puri, who always supported me as an older sibling and steered me in the right direction – and still does.

I thank Mum and Dad, who never stopped my dreams. They always supported everything I ever did, even when I was halfway across the world. And they have taken care of me so generously financially – a million times over.

I thank the many guides and mentors from whom I've learned love and patience. Vivek B. Gaur who told me to remain as I am.

And I thank the people who crossed my path in Bollywood/Hollywood. You were part of my self-growth. I thank you for that.

I thank all the love relationships in my life for truly caring for me and wishing to see me flourish. I thank everyone who comes to my meditations in Brampton. Thanks for your loyalty and believing in me.

I thank all the friends who I met over coffee. All the valuable advice and guidance they gave me. And my gratitude also goes out to the wonderful friends I made in
Niagara Falls – all the healers.

You guys welcomed me to your homes or studios and showed me so much love and   support when I wanted to do chakra meditation. Thank you.
My thanks also go out to my dear editors. I am so grateful they walked into my life. I gave them the "vomit version" of the book, and with their patience and skill, they put it together.

This book could not have come together if I had not had them to sort it out. Isis Pickens, who was the first set of eyes for this book, taught me to write better and always encouraged me with her kind words.

My second editor, Doreen Zeitvogel, always gave me more than her two bits to bring out the best in me. She has such great energy, this woman – I'm just inspired by seeing how she operates.

My gratitude also to my cheerful photographer, John Triffo, who did the book cover. I am so thankful for this easygoing guy who never complains.

And I thank Sean Bridge for creating my website, for his techy mind and for helping me learn about e-commerce – and for so much more. I thank Isabela Rivas for transforming my vision into artwork for my website logo – and with such ease. No fuss, just love.

Once again, I thank you all and send you my love and light!

Being raised Indian isn't always so easy. Well, it wasn't for me, anyhow. You need a will of steel to keep back the commenters and brainwashers. Indian people have so many expectations. That wasn't really true of my parents, but it's true of the culture itself. And my parents would at times get sucked into these expectations, which would then affect me.

I never had the usual problems other Indian kids had. Their parents were constantly drilling them: "What university do you want to go to?" "What do you want to be?" "You should go for another degree. What you've got is not enough." Those were not the problems I had. I guess it helped that my parents never went to university – well, my father didn't, anyhow. He had always worked very hard from a young age. He knew what it meant to work, and in his mind, any kind of work was fine. As long as it paid the bills and put food on the table, that was plenty. A couple of his siblings went to university, but I guess my father didn't have a passion for university studies, so he never pushed university on me. Neither did my mother. Perhaps my parents knew I had no interest, so they didn't bother trying. Plus, money was always tight in our home, so maybe my lack of interest was a blessing in disguise for them and me, as we didn't have to dish out thousands of dollars per year on university fees.

My mother, however, did attend university. She had a B.A. in History from the University of Delhi. I suppose a B.A. degree in India was a big deal back in my mother's time in the mid-1960s. She tells me about it every day. I can understand how it must have been a real triumph for her and her siblings to reach such heights. She's definitely proud of that B.A. degree. It was also a lot for a single mother, as hers was, to put several children through university.

A lot of the credit and thanks go to my grandfather, whom I never met. My mother's father was the senior stationmaster of the railway department in East Africa from the 1930s to the mid-1950s. He worked for the railway for twenty years. That's where my mum and her siblings were raised, in East Africa for five years. Her father was doing very well in Africa, too. They constantly had to move from one part of the region to another, but all their comforts and needs were well taken care of. They had cooks and cleaners and all-around servants. My grandfather earned excellent pay, and their home had been given to them by the British government. One of my grandfather's servants would lead him to the railway station at night. It was very dark, and they were constantly surrounded by lions guarding their front porch. I have been told that the lions never harmed them, but they did have to watch out for these big cats hanging around. When my grandfather passed away because of malaria, he left all his wealth to his wife, my grandmother, whom I also never met, and she used the money to send a few of her children to university back in India. They left East Africa in the mid-1950s, since they had no reason to be there anymore, and they moved to India.

Life in India for my mum and her siblings was all about them – herself, her five siblings and their widowed mother. They didn't have time for gossip or parties and other celebrations. Nor did they have time for the neighbours. They just enjoyed their own intimate company.

My mother led a simple life – playing at home, going to the movies with her sisters, taking long walks. Then, of course, they liked to mess around with their mum, too, teasing her and playing with her. My mum enjoyed growing plants and flowers, and she still does. I suppose it was her simple ways and beauty that got her an extra role in a British film called *Nine Hours to Rama*. Shot in India and the UK in the early 1960s, it was a controversial film about the nine hours leading up to the assassination of Mahatma Gandhi. She played Godse's child-wife. All she had to do was be like a sleeping beauty – that was her scene. She enjoyed the experience of getting ready at the five-star Ashok Hotel in Delhi for three days and nights of shooting and being around a British film crew. The director suggested she come to Britain to become an actress, but my mother's family was somewhat strict and declined the suggestion.

Life got tough for my mum and her siblings when they moved back to India. Their mother had become very weak. She was in her dying stages. My mum's brothers took on their father's role as best they knew how, and my mum and her sisters did the cooking, housework, and so on. But the thing my grandmother was most proud of was that she got to see a few of her kids go to university.

As a family, we come from an interesting mix of soils. Each of us was born in a different country, and we finally settled on Canadian soil. My father was born in Lahore, Pakistan before the partition between India and Pakistan. My mum was born in East Africa, and my brother and I were both born in Delhi, India. Both my parents have fascinating backgrounds. My grandfather, my dad's dad, ran away from home when he was in the tenth grade to embark on the path of the Divine. He wanted to be a saint. He left right in the middle of his school day. After he ran away, the children reported it to his parents, my great grandparents, and brought him back home. They soon got him married to steer him away from the spiritual path.

Possibly because of their interesting backgrounds, my parents never felt the need to mingle much with others in the Indian community. That's probably why I always had the freedom to do my own thing, too. My parents never got too caught up in what's expected of Indian people. And even if they knew it, we never really followed any of it. We're somewhat of a black-sheep family that strayed off on its own ventures.

EARLY YEARS-WINTERPEG

My life has had so much freedom. I have my parents to thank for that. And it started when I first arrived in this world. I guess I decided not to come out headfirst, the way everyone else does. I was a breech baby. My feet landed on this planet first.

I haven't always felt grounded. In fact, my life has been everything but that. My feet may have landed on the planet first, but they just couldn't stay put. I've moved here and there, with and without my family. For these feet, travelling was about freedom. These feet were meant to walk. And I have had nothing but freedom in my life to walk, jog or run. Nobody, including my parents, has ever stopped my feet. Many of my crazy moves in life have not been accepted, but nobody ever tried to stop these feet from jumping if I wanted them to.

Today I really appreciate what freedom is. I am also free in how I spend my day. I have ample free time in this world at the moment. I keep asking the Divine Energies: what do you want me to do with such a minimal weekly schedule? How am I supposed to survive? How can I earn money? I have to pay bills like everyone else. How come you send me only a four-hour work schedule? The answer I got was: Write. Devote your energies and most of your time to writing. I've never read the book *The 4-Hour Work Week*, but that's kinda my work schedule. The rest of the time I write.

Early Childhood

I can remember as far back as when I was three-and-a-half years old. We lived in a three-story home that was a fair size. Considering my parents were immigrants to a new country, they did all right. We lived in the heart of the city on Toronto Street in downtown Winnipeg. Coincidentally, I moved to Toronto many, many years later.

I remember a lot about that particular home at age three. On the top floor, one bedroom was rented out to an older gentleman who would mostly keep to himself. I would stand at the bottom of the stairs just staring, looking up at his door and wondering when he would open it to come out ... but nothing. So I carried on being a kid. We only saw him once in a blue moon – it was very rare to see him come in and out.

I grew up in Winnipeg in the late '70s. Winnipeg is a small prairie city in Canada – very Anglo-Saxon Caucasian. It has extreme weather conditions, very cold winters and very hot summers. I come from a family of four – my mother, father, an older brother who passed away years ago, and me. He was four years my senior. Now it's just the three of us. There were many trying periods in my life growing up.

I can clearly remember, when I was three years old, floating above my bed in sukhasan. I'll never forget it. I can't recall how long this went on, but I was floating long enough that it made an impact on my future life. I was gently placed back on my bed, still with my legs crossed in sukhasan.

Next I remember I was standing on the floor, still in my bedroom, and this beautiful majestic figure appeared in front of me. I remember the whole room was illuminated. He was a godlike figure – tall, with a long white beard – but I was not frightened. I felt secure in his presence. He put a smooth rock in my hand, closed my fist around it and said, "Keep this with you." I looked up and nodded in a way that said, "Yes, sir." I remember waking up the next day to see if the rock was still there – and it was! I put it in a little red money pouch I had, and for years it never left my side. We even moved homes, and I still had it with me and would for a long time. I looked at it every now and then to recollect the memory of that day. But then, years later, when I was around thirteen or fourteen years old, I lost my special rock that I'd put in my little red money pouch.

That was the age when I discovered boys and started dating. The innocence of childhood was gone, and because of that, the experience I'd had with the enlightened figure at age three slowly started to dissolve from my memory, and I lost the little red money pouch with that precious piece of nature. I long for it now and still sometimes hope it will reappear somehow. I started to block my memory of that spiritual experience I'd had when I was three years old by trying to convince myself that it wasn't real. When you live in the everyday so-called real world, you become it, and there was no way back for me at that time.

Still, even as a teenager, I was ready to express how I was just a little different. One fine day, as I was reading *Autobiography of a Yogi* by Paramahansa Yogananda, I was able to rejoice in faith and hope again. There was a chapter in there that talked about the atom of the Omnipotent appearing anytime and anywhere to whatever individual was blessed to see the vision. After I read that chapter and more of his autobiography, it all came back to me – the time when I was three and the Omnipotent presented itself to me!

If I had to make a comparison, I would say that the figure somewhat resembled Osho. I discovered Osho when I was about thirty-four. I was really drawn to him for some reason – perhaps because of my earlier experience. But I am now confident that what I saw when I was three was the beautiful Omnipotent. And three has always been my number. Isn't that interesting? Another of the fun-filled puzzles of the Divine. It's great to put the pieces together when you become enlightened.

Upbringing

As a child, I was a bit aloof, a bit different. I never really fit in with anyone. I loved to be in nature, to just be on my own, in my own zen. I remember one time when I was playing in the park near the lake at age seven. I found a bird with a broken wing. I picked it up and brought it home to nurture it. Today, as a yogini spiritual being, the world is my nurturing ground. I know things now with great clarity and vividness that as a child were just one big blur.

When you are young, you don't really know what it is that makes you different. You just know that something about you is different from other children, but you can't pinpoint how you are different. I was a spiritual soul who was present and engrossed in Mother Nature, always observing it. I took my sweet time walking to school. My elementary school was far from home, and at that time, I had to walk to whatever schools there were. There was hardly ever a soul in sight, so most of the time I walked alone – just me, walking and breathing in the natural beauty all around me. I never minded it, though. I could spend all day walking outside. I wasn't in any hurry to hit the books at school.

I easily forget that nobody is quite like me. Well, none of us are the same, anyhow. We all have something unique about us that makes us stand out in our own right. For myself, I get reminded of who I am when I meet new people or have intimate conversations with others. For one thing, I never grew up under normal conditions. In that sense, I can see that I am different from everyone I meet. I especially notice it in my lovers because of the amount of time I spend with them and because I get to know their innermost thoughts. They all have an innocence about them that comes from the way they were raised – family values, upbringing, etc. They all have a certain fear of their families, and they feel that they owe them some kind of respect. That's very foreign to me. I don't feel I owe anyone anything.

I never had any family values instilled in me. But I get it now – that was the way it was supposed to be. I spent most of my kid years in my room. I would spend hours and hours alone there. No one would even come and ask about me. They, too, were absorbed in their own thing. Nobody had any idea what I was doing in there. My parents were really in a world of their own. I don't blame them in a way. They were immigrants to a new country and had to take care of the house and the bills and put food on the table. It was enough for them to just worry about the normal provisions, so they just let us kids be to figure things out for ourselves. We all lived under the same roof, but we were in different worlds. My brother did his own thing, I did my own thing, and my parents had a lot of domestic disputes – that was their thing.

Financial shortfalls also added to a constant sense of struggle. I remember once eating at a food court with my Mum, and she wouldn't eat because there wasn't enough money in her purse, so she let me have whatever I wanted and just sat across from me at the table, keeping me company. She sacrificed her own meal to feed her child. She was so full of kindness and compassion towards me. She didn't complain but just smiled.

Home wasn't exactly a place of learning. However, I've always been fortunate. From a young age, I have mostly learned everything from the outside world of friends and lovers. It's been a path and pattern in my life. I take the good I learn from everything around me and achieve a positive way of thinking from it.

I was pretty much on my own from the get-go. I always found things to do. I never felt bored. I was happy to be my own solace, and I was happy to be in my own reclusive world. Today I live my life exactly the same way. I'm happy to keep to myself, do my yoga, meditate and do other things I enjoy. Being on my own has been my innate way since childhood. I never talked to people much. I think I was more of an observer even at a young age. Instead, I kept my thoughts to myself, and there was a lot going on in this little brain. There still is, but the beauty now is that there is also stillness – just empty space … it's bliss.

If my judgment is not off, my brother was the same way. He, too, was able to quiet his mind, to find peace in stillness. We were both eccentric, finding the world on our own for the most part. We fought like cats and dogs, like any other siblings on this planet, but we were close, too. We would look to each other for comfort and for the simple joys in life, and our little sibling fights were just our way of showing love and affection. I don't think we have any regrets.

I became my own person at a fairly young age from the loss of my brother when I was sixteen. That was when life changed. I didn't feel it so much at the time – I was a rebellious wild child. But in my own way, I was dealing with the loss through rebellious behaviour. I am and forever will be first the child of the Divine. I give my parents the love they deserve, but my highest regard and love is for the Infinite. Watching domestic disturbances from the age of three and then suffering the loss of my brother when I was sixteen left me truly alone. But I am not alone, because the world has become my children, and I will preach to it about us as spiritual beings. That is what I am sent here to do. That is my birth purpose. The Infinite is my greatest true friend, my lover, my solace, my father, my mother – the Infinite is everything to me. He had a hold on me from age three, and I knew it.

My first spiritual dilemma happened when I was seven. Back then my best friend was a lanky pale redhead. We got along great and were inseparable in those days. I slept over at her house nearly every weekend. One particular weekend, we awoke on a Sunday morning, and her parents announced that we were going to church. I was brought up in a traditional Indian household, with Indian gods. I had never been to a Christian church before. There was a bit of commotion about what to do with the little Indian girl. I was pretty calm about the whole thing. She and I were like sisters, and her family was like family to me. They treated me with the same love they showed my friend. So there I was, going to church with my friend's family.

Once we got to the church, I became a little nervous. "The priest is going to come around with a little round white chip," my friend whispered to me. "Make sure you don't eat it." Her words made me curious. "Why shouldn't I eat it?" I thought. "What would happen if I did?" I knew it had something to do with religion, and I thought it might be because I wasn't white. I shook my head to signal OK to my friend. But then, as the priest came closer, I grew very excited. *I want to eat it*, I thought. I could probably get away with sneaking a small bite. A brief tinge of doubt began forming in my mind. *If I ate it, would the priest kick me out of the church?* Or would he say, *"Hey, who let the Indian girl take the chip?"* Maybe he'd scream, *"What are you doing here?"* when he saw me eating it. These thoughts raced through my seven-year old mind.

So the priest came around, and the time came to take the little white chip. My heart was pounding as he drew closer to me. I watched to see what all the others were doing. Then the moment arrived, and the priest was standing right in front of me. I looked up at him and I put my hand out, as I had seen the others do. He placed that little white chip in my hand – and I ate it! I really ate it! And you know what? Nothing bad happened. Everything was fine. I felt kind of special. I felt very safe. I felt honoured to be in church, in a place where God is worshipped. It's a moment I'll never forget. Maybe I was feeling a sense of spirituality.

But what did it all mean? If God knew separation, if God only loved those who took a specific religion, how could I, the little Indian girl, feel so special that day? If God saw separation, I would not have made it that day. Surely something would have happened. Some unexpected incident would have hindered me from getting to church with my friend, right?

That was a moment of truth for me. I needed to spend the night with my friend that weekend and join her family in church that Sunday. It was all so I could realize the beauty of God's Love. Until that moment, I only knew the love of the gods in my own household – gods like Krishna and the others represented in Indian culture. But at the church, with my friend and the priest, a different god named Jesus came into my life. The Jesus I met knew no difference between cultures. He knew only that I needed a connection to him. And so, we connected

21

purely and truly.

We need to understand that there is only one Omnipotent, One Supreme Divine Light. But we also need to be careful not to limit ourselves to only one representation of that Divine Light. God is in all things and is represented whenever and wherever there is holy Light.

My mum's a lovely woman, but she can be a worrywart. Still, her worries come from a place of love. I do get it, but in my opinion, too much thinking is no good for anybody, and she thinks way too much for her own good. She cogitates about all sorts of crazy things. Mother can also be a very stubborn person. It's hard to get her out of her thoughts, so I don't try. I just let her be. I am more or less entertained by it now. And sometimes she ends up laughing with me when she realizes how silly she's being. My mother can be a kind soul, and she's usually received well by others. She treats everyone with kindness and respect. So when she's not behaving in a bull-like way, I appreciate her good traits. When people come over for meditation practice with me, they definitely like to greet my mother before starting or after finishing their meditation. She has a very calming demeanour about her that is soothing for them.

My father can be stubborn, too. Actually all three of us can be. Everybody has their days when they're a bull on the throne. But can you imagine living with two very stubborn people? Still, mum and dad have a really great sense of humour. My father loves to crack jokes at parties, and everyone loves his cheerfulness. He is always the loudest one at the party. At home he's a pretty quiet guy. At home, Dad and I usually joke around at my mother's expense. But it's all good. My dad and I get into fights, too ... oh yes, we do! It's usually when he's being irrational and not seeking love in the right way. It can upset the household as it would any home. But after a few hours, everything is usually back to normal again. And that's the way love goes!

I have seen this kind of thing a lot on his side of the family. It runs in the genes on his side –they can be melodramatic. Everyone wants love, but some don't seek it in the right way. But over the years, I've slowly but surely been seeing positive changes in my father.

My dad is an old-timer. He sees the youth of today spending their money like they pulled it out of a hat. But he operates his life in a more resourceful manner – hold on to what you have because you never know when you'll need it. Actually, to tell you the truth, I'm the same way. Perhaps I've learned it through osmosis. I also understand where Dad gets his thinking. It's part of the culture he was raised in in India. In India, people don't throw anything out. Basically, the whole country likes to hoard. My father was raised in India at a time when you never knew when the electricity was going to go out, so you always had old candles around that you never threw out. Every item you ever bought came in handy at some point or other. There was no wasting anything. He still holds that same mentality here in Canada – hold onto your cash, your stuff. You never know when you'll need it.

I suppose I have a special relationship with my father. We don't say a lot to each other but we communicate through our actions. Both my parents spoil me with *huge* unconditional love. I'm a full-grown adult but they still don't let me pay for anything. The other day I had to get my wisdom tooth pulled out. I knew it was going to cost me a big chunk of money, so I saved up well in advance. I work for myself, which is great, but that means I don't have my dental expenses covered for me. It was a pretty decent bill, and dad paid it for me. I knew that was a lot for him. I insisted that he let me pay. I already had it saved up, anyhow. But he just would not let me pay. He said, "It's okay. Save it for your book expenses." I know I'm lucky to have the comforts of a nice home and two loving parents. Sometimes I feel that's the only reason I can do what I do. If I had to be out there struggling to pay for rent and trying to achieve my creative goals at the same time, it would be a lot harder. This roof over my head is giving me time to really build myself. Thanks, Mum and Dad. Your love and care is another proof to me of how the Divine has always swept me in his light.

Parental Thoughts

I want to put in some words about my opinion about my daughter

My daughter likes travelling. Anywhere where she can see the beautiful ocean and mountains she likes a lot.

In my opinion, work is hard labor that everyone should do in their lifetime. In my opinion, I don't think my daughter did much of that kind of work. She would never go and get a job at McDonald's. I told her, "There nothing wrong with it," but she didn't like labor jobs like that.

She likes everything clean. She gets mad at us – me and my wife – if everything is not cleaned. She needs cleanliness all the time. No matter if it's the car or house or what!

From a young age, she always desired to see new people and become new friends with them. She likes interesting people, and that's why she ended up in Bollywood for two years. She makes friends all over the world.

She cannot take criticism. She gets mad if you tell her anything.

She doesn't waste time. If she wants to do something, she does it right away.

From a very young age, she is always thinking big and expensive for things like clothing, shoes, car.

Once upon a time, all my family was at my home – all my brothers and sisters were there. And one of my nephews saw a picture of Charu sitting very high on the shelf. And he asked me, "Uncle, why did you put this picture very high on the shelf?" And I said, "I want to see my daughter one day on top of the world."

She has a very kind heart towards the people she meets, but not towards the family. To the family, she is different.

As a father, I was watching her all I can, how she is growing. But I don't know when it happened that suddenly I saw her become a yogi, then modern yogi, and then she got enlightened. This is a surprise in my life.

She's the apple of my eye, but you have to have that kind of eye to see her. But I don't have that, because I'm seeing her as a daughter.

Your Papa

Most respectfully, I'm going to express a few thoughts towards my daughter. These thoughts have always come to my mind since she was a child – that this baby must be very special for the family as well as for me. When she was born, it was a bright morning sun and blue clear skies. And the night before was a very bright moon.

From the very childhood age, she always had high thoughts and simple living. And she likes high taste in all the things, too. I would tell my husband maybe she was like princess in previous life.

Even though she is very simple, she is always kind to needy people by giving shelter and food to them. Whatever the looks of the person, she trusts easily and brings the person home to give maximum comforts as she can.

She has very tender heart and believes easily on them, even if the person is cheater. If she knew that in later time the person did harm to her, she still forgive them.

One day, one pigeon came to our backyard, and it was very hard for the bird to fly. She start giving her full attention to the bird by giving it drops of water to survive. He was hungry and thirsty. Finally, after three or four hours of spending time on the bird to do the hard work so he can fly, he still could not. But she took lots of pictures of the bird for memory. And she phoned the bird care department to take the bird and care for it.

Now I am thinking my daughter is my best friend as well as a good helper in my old age. She is caring for me more than any other child would. I am proud of my God's gift child, which I love. She's my son, my daughter. Sometimes she cooks the food when I am sick. She shops for me and does groceries for me. She is a well-wisher for me, too. She always thinks positive for me. She never thinks negative.

She's very straightforward. She never hides if she feels the person has some good qualities but the person is doing wrong. She gives the good advice to improve him or her. She always brings the truth in front of the thing. That's why people love her from the bottom of their hearts.

In a spiritual way, I see she is gaining her popularity, slowly, slowly.

In her character, she has good morals and high thinking and good dignity. She is leading a simple life and eating simple food, which makes her healthy and gives her a slim, attractive body. I know that she is very charming and beautiful, and any person can easily fall in love with her. But she has a very strong determination for life.

26

She has good activities. Even when she did a big dive from a big waterfall in the movie she was shooting in Mauritius when she was in film, she did not have any safety equipment on, and she did it still.

May God bless her for a happy, successful, prosperous and healthy life. And may God give her full strength in every step of her life.

Your well-wisher and loving mum

School Days

When I think back to my school days, I remember that school was really hard for me through all the grades – from the first day of first grade to the last day of high school. I don't know how I got through it. I was never really there. I always lived in a world of my own. Mostly, I spent my time at school studying my teachers' psyches. Why did they look so tired? What kind of families did they have? Did they really enjoy teaching us? Those were the thoughts that went through my mind during class. In the end, I failed first grade because of this absent-mindedness I had during the school day.

I almost failed high school, but I made up some bullshit that I came from a very traditional household, and now that I was eighteen, my parents were going to send me to India to get married … so please, I need this high school diploma – don't keep me back another year. I had to beg my math teacher, because it was his final grade that would make or break me, since I just barely passed every other subject. If he failed me, I would have to spend another year in high school. I don't think he believed me, not even for a second.

I'm not sure why he passed me. I think he felt sorry for me because I was going through such extreme measures to pass. Also, the whole school knew that I was the girl whose brother had committed suicide a couple of years back when I was in tenth grade at the same high school. So I'm sure my wonderful math teacher was empathetic and decided to grant me a passing mark. To this day, I still have nightmares about whether I actually passed high school or not, and in the dreams, I still have to go back and complete it.

After reading *Autobiography of a Yogi,* I was inspired to know that Paramahansa Yogananda Ji also had no interest in his studies. He did not like school and preferred to constantly be in the company of his master Sri Yukteswarji. His master explained to him, "Yes, Paramahansa, you do not like school because you are a student of the enlightened world, which is a different kind of study altogether. You will learn all about subjects taught in regular schools, but you will learn these subjects through the teachings of yoga and meditation. They will teach you all about the subjects of this world and its countries." However, at his master's request, Paramahansa did go to university and get a degree in order to prepare himself to deal with the North American countries.

I relate to Paramahansa in some ways. I, too, never liked school. The world is my school. I learn each and every day from situations, people, things, experiences. I would like, however, to learn more about science, as I always try to integrate science into my way of teaching yoga and meditation. But spirituality and science can be enemies. The scientist searches outwardly for the answers, while the yogi searches inwardly. They are both looking for the same thing, though.

Following my school years, as I now entered my adult phase, I was still touchy and shaky. I had to find my own way. In my early twenties and into my thirties, I kept meeting guides, gurus, mentors, saints and astrologers. These people just entered my life. I never asked for them. They just showed up somehow, and they all said the same thing to me: "You will be globally known." I never quite believed them and thought, "Well, how will that be possible?" Because my life was heading nowhere – there was no direction. I had been a lost soul for most of my life. Only now are their sayings making more sense to me, and that's because I have a vision of how I want to help people through my enlightened experience. I can now share this knowledge with everyone. My hope is that my words will somehow leave an impact and that I can give that light to the world. Perhaps I have more trust today in what these wonderful mentors had to say.

Flashback: The Unimaginable

It was the hardest, most bone-chilling sight I ever saw. I was sixteen. It was a normal day at school. I remember the sun was out, and it was a bright day. When I came home, I saw my mum crouched down, leaning against the kitchen patio door, bawling her eyes out. I thought to myself, "Huh, here we go again. My brother and her probably had one of their usual fights, and now she's so upset she's crying against the wall." But something was different about her tears this time. She was howling and shrieking. I knew something wasn't right, but I kept my cool. Finally, I couldn't take her howling anymore. It was piercing my ears. So I asked her in an annoyed but casual tone, "What's wrong with you? Why are you crying so much?" All she could say was, "Your brother, your brother, upstairs. The tub. Go see the tub. Your brother, upstairs."

I knew I was about to face something unimaginable. I slowly made my way up the stairs. I was still trying to keep cool, but my legs were shaking. I held onto the staircase railing for support and called my brother's name several times: "Neil! Neil!" He didn't answer. As I got closer to the top of the stairs, I noticed the light beige-coloured carpet had weird stuff all over it. I couldn't make out what it was, but all this stuff – it didn't look right. I glanced at the white hallway walls, which were splashed with red. I called Neil's name again. Still no answer. I was getting annoyed and angry. "Neil! This isn't funny. This isn't funny, you know!" Still no response. He liked to spook me, so I assumed this was some kind of sick trick. I looked down again, still not understanding what I was stepping on. It was just this weird stuff. As I made it up to the final step, I stopped for a second and called his name again. Nothing. I was expecting him to pop out from around the corner and say "Gotcha!" By now, my whole body was numb, and my heart was racing. I slowly kept walking, turning right at the hallway. Just a few inches down the hallway was the bathroom. As I got closer, the splashes of red on the hallway walls intensified. There was a lot of red everywhere. And the stuff on the ground was everywhere, too – plenty of it. I was stepping all over it. I called his name again. This time I got so angry I was aggressive. "Neil! Neil! Seriously, this is not funny!" I slowly crept up to the bathroom door as I got closer to it. I saw the bathroom wall was covered in red. The same stuff from the floor was all over the bathroom walls, too.

I never went into the bathroom. I couldn't. I was too numb to move. My heart was pounding. But I did pop my head in. That was when I screamed. My legs were like rubber as I tried to make my way down the stairs. I mostly slipped and tumbled down. I realized that stuff I was tumbling on was skin, bones and brains. My brother had taken his own life. Of course, I would have liked to see him leave naturally from this planet, but he was excited to get to the spirit world quick. It's okay. He's a happy soul, and his love shines down on me every day.

It all started coming back to me now. All the things he taught me, his yogi attitude, everything was flashing in front of me. I remembered asking him, "Where are you going? How come you're not coming back?" I even remember the daunting day he brought that big rifle into the house in a big duffle bag. I happened to catch him coming into the house with the duffle bag. He tried to sneak it in, but I saw it. I asked him, "What's in there?" I knew something wasn't right. Now it was all flashing before my mind's eye.

My mum was still on the ground, wailing and crying out his name. I was calm. I just stood there, watching her, feeling her pain. Then my father came home. He had no idea what was going on. All I could think was, "My poor dad is going to get the shock of his life." He looked frightened as he asked, "What is going on? What is all the chaos about?" My mum told him, "Nidhu, Nidhu – upstairs." Nidhu was Neil's home name. Still not understanding, my dad went up to see what was going on. I heard him scream from upstairs. He came down crying, trying to stay strong and calm for my mum and me. He called the police. They were in our home, taking notes and all. My parents were in no condition to speak. I was the only one who was calm enough to hold a conversation with them.

I wasn't going to write about this. I actually only added it in the final days of putting the book together. But something told me it was okay to talk about it. It's an integral part of who I am. This was the most profound experience of my life. It's the reason I'm here today, doing what I do. It was my brother's wish to see me grow in life and express myself. And he would not want me to leave any expression out, especially considering that I would always say to him, "You should express yourself." Whenever we would have our sibling arguments, I would say to him, "You should express yourself. Say what you feel." I don't really think I knew what I was saying back then. But for some reason, I used to say that to him.

My brother is probably surprised to know that I'm writing. He used to make fun of my English all the time. I remember I used to say, "Do you member that time? Member, member?" He used to correct me. "It's not 'member', stupid, it's RE-member." I had lots of word pronunciation issues, and he would constantly correct me on them. He taught me humbleness, too. I would behave snotty to most people I met, and he'd say, "If you keep that up, you're not gonna have any friends when you're older. You should learn how to treat people properly." He would also definitely let me know if he thought I wasn't dressed appropriately for a young teenager. I was quite the little Miss Thing. He had to keep me in check most of the time. For my sixteenth birthday, he bought me a beautiful white dress to wear for my Sweet Sixteen party that my parents were throwing me. It was so sophisticated, this dress – all white, with a little bit of lace on the shoulders. But I thought to myself, "It's nice, but it's too sophisticated. He's making me look like a lady." I couldn't believe he picked it out for me and surprised me with it. He really went out of his way for my birthday. "Here, this is your birthday present. You can wear it to your party." I remember pulling it out of the big box.

I was pretty surprised. I had no words at first. I said, "This is for me? This is mine?" But then I kept thinking it was too "old person"-looking. When I put it on, though, I fell in love with it. It looked so nice! It really worked on me. I looked like a classy sixteen-year-old girl. He knew better than I did what I would look good in.

Of all the people in my life who are gone now, my brother is the most valuable to me. He's one of my soulmates. He taught me so much in his own subtle way. I didn't start to miss him until a good ten years after his passing. As a young adult, it all started to kick in. That's when I felt the most alone, when I had to learn life on my own and find strength from somewhere within. I would see that strength in the people I met, and I thought it was because everyone I met had at least one sibling. And I saw how having even one sibling in their lives gave a lot of people so much comfort that seemed to just come naturally. And you only really know the value of it once it's gone. It's the small things you miss most, like being able to call your brother and ask him about problems you're having with your car. Or pairing up on discounted insurance together, or on family cell phone plans. Or if you're having a tech issue with your home theatre setup or your camcorder, or with your home reno stuff, your bro could come over and help you. I also used to think that people with siblings got to hang out with them whenever they wanted, in case they didn't feel like seeing their friends. I missed hanging out with my buddy. Sometimes at home it was tough handling my fighting parents, too. It hit me that I'd taken over the role he left me with. I used to curse my brother at times: "Why did you leave me all alone to deal with them?" But the message he kept giving me then – and still does now – was to take care of my parents as best I could. Even when they fought, I had to take care of them. *Take care of mum and dad.* My strength comes from Neil. He lives deep within me. I emulate many things I know he would do as a son. I am a boy. I am a girl. I have no complaints about these roles. They have taught me life.

I remember the week my brother passed away. My parents were in mourning, and a lot of people came to our home to give us their condolences. Even if my parents had wised up to the fact that they didn't have to be in mourning, they still had to act like they were for the sake of all those people who kept coming into the house and expecting to see them that way.

I'm not sorry when someone dies. In fact, I won't say, "I'm sorry to hear that." I feel compassion for them, and I know it's a sad time, but if you think in spiritual terms, the person has gone off to another realm and is experiencing new surroundings. When you know that there is no death, and you know that only the body died and that the person's soul or spirit lives on, that thought frees you from feeling the need to mourn.

A lot of times, we're conditioned to do things because people expect it. But that doesn't make it right. It's just what's expected. And if they don't see it, it causes a storm. Well, I caused a storm. I was not in the conventional state of mourning that my family, friends, aunts and uncles expected to see. In fact, I was still able to laugh, smile and crack jokes. Oh, my... You should have seen the looks I got. But I knew better. I knew in my heart and soul that I was in mourning for my brother Neil. It's just that I had to do it in my own way, in private. It was not to be displayed in public for the sake of people's expectations. So while I was among them, I showed strength. I showed hope. I showed that I could still laugh and smile and live my life, even though I'd had a loss. They didn't get it. They looked at me like I was cold.

I think there was only one aunt who understood my silence, who knew I didn't need to make a show of my emotions. I remember I had my head down. It was just a moment of going within myself. Next thing I knew, my head was being pressed into someone's thighs. The person was standing right up against me, so I couldn't see who it was. I stayed in that position, sitting on the couch with my head caressing the person's thighs as whoever it was stood there comforting me. When the person's grip finally loosened, I looked up to see who it was – this sensible person who really got me, who really understood what I was going through. It was my aunt, the only one in the room who heard what was behind my silence and embraced it. And she caressed me with her own silence and her love. She saw that I was just *being*.

When you feel that you have to come up with some rote statement, you're left with an awkward scenario that could have been handled in a more compassionate or spiritual manner. The mood is ruined, when instead you could have taken the person higher, to a place of spiritual peace. A loving silence, for example, has the power to make an experience a moving and profound one. Instead of an awkward conversation, there can be a deep, smooth interaction, like the movement of the wind and trees silently swooshing together.

Shouting Out To Neil's Friends

I remember a few of Neil's close friends. I just wanna say to them, if any of you end up reading or knowing about this book, I'd love to meet or at least have a conversation with you, just to say hello. It would be nice for us to exchange a few words about Neil and our memories of him. So I'm reaching out to Ken, the white guy. I remember you came over to the house a lot. Then there's Tony, the black guy. I remember you were always happy, smiling, with nice big white teeth. I know that Ken and Tony did a few camping trips with Neil. I have one or two pictures of them. There was also Lyle, who worked with Neil at Pizza Hut, I think. I know you guys had a big falling out, but I would love to hear from you, anyhow. You know ... how's life, etc. Vanessa, you were pretty and slim – you had a South American or Italian look. I think you were pretty close to Neil, too. I would love to hear from all of you. Just to say hello. And, of course, if there are any others out there who were my brother's friends that I didn't know about, even girlfriends or something, I'd love to hear from you. I know my brother was a good-looking guy. Some people say he looked like Billy Ray Cyrus. I think so too, actually. I know there were girls, anyhow. I remember a picture of one. Very pretty girl from Hawaii or Trinidad or somewhere. She was wearing a summer dress and had a flower in her hair. I would love to talk to you, too. I'm reaching out to all of you. It's just my way of remembering him when he was in a physical form – and of being close to him. That's all.

VANCOUVER

I never spent much time around any aunts or uncles growing up. We were in Winterpeg, as we called it, meaning Winnipeg. My grandparents, my dad's parents, raised my brother and me for some years, but only until I was around ten years old. So I didn't have much in the way of family influences, and neither did my parents. It wasn't until much later in my life, in my adult years, that some of these influences started coming into play.

After we left Winnipeg, we lived in Vancouver, Canada, for some years. Vancouver was not one of my great life chapters. It's where I left my short-lived marriage. It was a good thing we broke up – I have no issues with it. It's funny how you forget a lot of the past when you move forward with your life. I've forgotten most of the period when I was married in Vancouver.

After Vancouver, we moved to Toronto. All that moving my family did within Canada had mostly to do with the loss of my brother. We kept moving from one place to the next to find peace. I think it made us vulnerable at times, and we lost a lot of money from all the moving from house to house and city to city. There was also a lot of internal pain and confusion within each of us. Maybe in our weakened condition we were easily influenced by others in the Indian community. But by then I was already thinking, "Who cares about what others are doing? I don't really care. I'm an adult in my tough twenties. I'll make my own choices. They're not always going to be the right choices, but I have to find out for myself." That was the way I saw it. I didn't want to listen to who was doing what, or to go to school for this or that, or to get married, etc. But my parents somehow let the pressures of being Indian get to them. I suppose I let them get to me also. I made many wrong choices – but no regrets. It's because of all that stuff that I am where I am today.

I was foolish to get married at twenty-three. I hadn't had that much life experience, yet there I was, ready to take on a marriage. In fact, I still don't know if it's for me, but I definitely was not ready back then. When we left Winnipeg for Vancouver, I was only twenty years old, and I met a guy there who soon became my boyfriend. Nice guy, but that's not enough for a serious committed relationship. Everything moved too fast, and within two years, I was married to him. Bad move – for everyone involved. We were just kids. We didn't know what the hell we were doing. It was just young foolish love. That short-lived marriage lasted no more than a year. I would do all kinds of things to sabotage it, and my efforts worked. I guess I really must have got caught up in all the Indian social pressures to make a dumb move like that. Good thing I have a bounce-back attitude towards life, because I managed to put it behind me and move on to the many chapters to come.

I don't let the pressures of being Indian get to me much anymore, because I know now that I am everything. I can happily be whatever I want or need to be, for myself or for others. But the community, the culture, always tries to mould you. So people would look at me like: "Why don't you get a real job?" "Why don't you work 9-5?" "Do you make enough money?" "How come you don't settle down with one person?" It's not a big deal, though. Just listen, be nice about it, and then do your own thing. I'd always think to myself, "I have a real job. It's real for me, even though it might not be real for you. And what I make is not a lot, but I manage to be comfortable, and I don't have debts or extra expenses." I've never actually had to say that to anyone. I don't need to justify myself. But I think it, and they get the message. I can't help it if certain Indian people are used to being around successful engineers, IT professionals, pharmacists, doctors, MBAs or CAs. If you have any of these titles and you're Indian, you're considered to be totally on the right track in life. You're respected. But if you don't fit into any of these categories, you suck. You might get away with it if your spouse has some title. Then you're still in the game. You can still fit the Indian acceptability criteria. I'm just picking on a small percentage of the culture. I know not all Indian people are like this, but some of you out there know what I'm talking about.

As a successful Indian person, your home should be at least 2400 square feet, with a double garage and at least one high-end car. Well, I don't have most of those things. I have the car, but that didn't come easy and, of course, I have to work hard just like everyone else to pay for it. We had all the big beautiful houses, my family and I, but after we left Winnipeg, we could not maintain that lifestyle. All that moving around put my parents in a critical financial situation. But that's okay. My desire is to someday get them a beautiful home again. They actually won a big home back in the 1970s, in Toronto. They bought a lottery ticket and happened to win a big house. But they weren't able to accept it because they'd already planned to settle in Winnipeg instead of Toronto. So I would like that lottery ticket to come back for them again, and this time, I want it to be so the house is theirs to keep.

Indian weddings are lavish. If you've never been to an Indian wedding, you really have to check one out if you ever get the opportunity. Just make sure you're covered in dazzling jewels.

An Indian wedding is very pretty – a true ball for the prince and princess. I'm not just talking about the bride and groom. It's a ball for everyone there. However, there can be a lot of pressure when you attend an Indian marriage. For one thing, you have to be wearing gold, and one piece of gold doesn't cut it. That would make you kind of poor. In Indian culture, you are as rich as the amount of gold you have on. And what better place to show it off than at a lavish Indian wedding? That means earrings, bangles, necklaces, and rings. These days, diamonds are also the "in" thing, so you should be sporting one of the two. Showing up at an Indian wedding with almost no real jewellery is like showing up at a fancy party wearing jogging pants. You will get plenty of odd looks. You might as well not attend. Most of all, this applies to the ladies.

Then there is the elegant Indian outfit called a sari that costs a minimum of $400 to $500 – for a decent one, anyhow. And that's a modest price tag. For those who don't know, a sari is one long sheet of beautiful material, usually rich silk, that's wrapped around your body and worn like a fitted dress, and it's expected that you wear one to a wedding. And India is the home of silk and has the best silk sari fabrics in the world.

Women will usually accommodate themselves to most of the pressures of an Indian wedding. They prepare well in advance, a few months sometimes. They'll think about which sari to wear and which jewellery, shoes, and so on they need to match the sari. And that sari you just spent $500 bucks on? Well, forget about it for at least a couple of years. Throw it way back in your closet somewhere, because the other women will remember that you wore it and even which wedding you wore it to. You need to give it at least two years before you recycle it – that's if you want to save dishing out another 500 buckaroos down the road. Oh, and if you're not only attending the actual wedding but all the other events leading up to the big day, then you have to have several other outfits, which will also set you back some big bucks. And the same thing applies as for the sari, except that you can recycle the outfit after about one year, since you didn't wear it for the main event.

I've actually done the unthinkable with the saris I've worn to the weddings I've attended. I've worn my mother's. Yup. Yes, I did. The thing about saris is that they're like that golden piece of clothing that you never throw out. The sari never goes out of style. It lasts forever because of the expensive material it's made of. Well, that's what a sari is – an expensive silk from twenty years ago that you can still wear. They have all kinds of wonderful patterns and designs and flowers and different shades of colour. A lot of women keep their silk saris for years and years. And then they pull them out even fifteen years later, and they look as good as new, and the women still wear them well. And that's what I chose to do – to wear my mum's old but golden saris. So the upside is that if you do have your favorite saris that you spent a fortune on, at least you can continue wearing them for the rest of your living days. Or you can pass them on to your daughter, like my mum did.

So that's what I did. I took my favourite saris belonging to my mum, which she was happy to pass on to me. She told me she had worn them when she was younger and that if I liked them, I should take them. So I did, and I felt proud to wear my mum's saris. I revamped them to give them a lil' extra kick here and there, like fancy stitching on the arms or bottom border. And that's what I've worn to the weddings I've been invited to. Most Indian girls won't wear their mum's saris. In fact, I don't think any of them do. It's considered kind of cheap, like I couldn't go out and spend $500. To me it wasn't about the money. I honestly just liked her saris and thought what a waste to keep these folded up in a suitcase. I'm gonna start wearing them. And the old saris are beautiful. They're much richer than today's saris. The fabrics they're made of are of a much better quality, too. You cannot get saris in such rich silks and chiffons, anymore. Well, I guess you could if you spent some serious cash for them. But most people spend in the $500 range. And fortunately for me, my mum wore designs and materials I love – sheers and chiffons and silks. They hug your body very nicely, and the saris made of thin silks and chiffons give you a very slim look. I have gotten compliments wearing the oldies: "Where did you get that sari? The material is fabulous!" I proudly answer, "It's my mum's sari from way back in the day."

I figure, I look good in a sari. I know how to keep up with the fab Indian women. What more do they want? They do, though – they do want more. But uh-uh, I'm not getting pressured into things like having my hair done, wearing makeup galore and having earrings that hang down to my chin. A simple, elegant sari with some pearls and crystals for jewellery is more than enough for me, and I'm set for the Indian ball. The men have it pretty easy. They just put on a sharp suit, and they're done. I always try to remember that it's just a wedding. Let people say what they want. I let them flex their Indian-wedding muscles all they want. It's temporary, anyhow. After this, we all just go home. Indian weddings are pretentious, but I can do them as long as I do them my way. No expectations. I am very happy with all I have. I don't let their expectations bring me down. And I'm happy to encourage my family to not get caught up in cultural or community expectations, either.

I remember one incident at age twenty-three, when I was living in Vancouver and a friend of mine from Winnipeg came to visit me. At that age, I was all about drinking, smoking, etc. I hadn't quite hit my spiritual path yet. What happened to us that night made me realize that I have always been alert, always aware of my surroundings.

It was a cold, rainy night, and we weren't up for heading out to any wild parties, but we still thought it would be nice to get some coolers and hang out and chill. We chose to do this in my car, and we parked in a very dim parking lot. It was about 9 p.m. when we started. We must have been hanging out for a while, because the drinks were starting to hit us. I wanted to stay somewhat coherent so I could drive us back home safely. As we were drinking, laughing and chatting away, I started to get an eerie feeling. I remember I became very alert to our surroundings while still participating in the moment. Anyhow, we continued sitting in the car and carrying on a long while through the night.

All of a sudden, a young guy knocked on the car window on the passenger side, the side where my friend was sitting. She was about to open the window when I shouted, "No! Don't open it! I don't trust him!" My girlfriend said, "Aah, he probably just wants to get directions or something." Again I yelled, "Don't open the window!" I saw the fear on my girlfriend's face as she realized, "Okay, maybe you're right."

I quickly put the car in forward gear, and as I was doing so, the guy started to get aggressive. "Open it! Open the window!" As we took off, I looked in the rearview mirror and saw that he had a knife. I could see the sharp metal blade in the car's headlights. I told my friend "See? He had a knife." She said, "OMG, how did you know he wasn't right?" I said, "I just sensed it." We got home safely and never went to any parking lots again.

Wow, there have been so many guides, gurus, and yogis in my life's journey! I love them all for what each of them has taught me. Each guide was there for my journey to the next level. Sometimes they taught me, and sometimes I taught them. These guides and gurus have come and gone for fifteen years now, and so many of them have come just like that – they just sort of popped up in my life.

I remember the very first spiritual guide I had. I was about twenty-three, and he was my lovely neighbor in Vancouver, Canada. I was over at his house one day, and he pulled out this big book. I don't know what it was, but I think it was some kind of spiritual bible. He opened to a page and told me I would be some kind of teacher – I would be some kind of spiritual being. I never really accepted his valuable words, but they always stuck in my head. He definitely had an impact on me. I can't even get his words out of my head today, as I always remember that feeling of confusion and amazement they gave me. He asked me to come back again and see him so that he could talk more with me about the details. I said, "Sure – see you tomorrow", but I didn't show up. I was scared. Perhaps I knew it was going to be true and have an impact on me, but in my life at that time, I wasn't ready to hear it.

He saw me a couple of days later. I felt awkward seeing him. I knew he had been expecting me the other day. He said, "You didn't come by the other day. It's okay – I know why you didn't come." He said it again: "I know why you didn't come. You're not ready." I didn't know what to say. I felt guilty for not going, like I'd done something really wrong. But he knew I wasn't ready. It was obvious. He saw the way I was living. I couldn't hide it from him – we lived too close to each other. He saw my wildness in those days. I was into my party life, my late nights, my drinking, my boyfriends. I think he knew I was gonna be doing this for a while yet. So that was it – that was the end of the first encounter with the first spiritual guide of my life. I will never forget it, even though it was the first one and a long time ago.

The next one came into my life when I moved to Ontario. We were living in an area called Markham. I was working at a local call center, so not much was going on in my life, and I was feeling a little low. I used to take the car and go for short drives, just for a change of pace and to collect my thoughts – that kind of thing. Many times, I drove by this one place that was beautifully structured. It always caught my attention, but I never could figure out what the place was. It looked like a church, so I always thought it was. One day, something made me drive closer. There was a board that read Arya Samaj, so I realized that it wasn't a church but some kind of Indian temple. I lit up. I felt like I needed to go into a place like that – that it would make me feel better. I parked the car and went in. Not much was going on. It was kind of quiet, and there was nobody in sight, so I left.

I was out for one of my drives another time, and again I gravitated towards the Arya Samaj. I parked and made my way in. This time, there were people sitting in the main hall, so I sat down and listened to the preaching. The main priest, called a pandit, saw me, smiled and waved his hand at me to come and sit closer to him. I felt happy and quickly made my way up to the front. It was nice that he waved me down like we knew each other, like I'd been there many times. But this was the first time we had ever seen each other, so it felt very welcoming.

After the preaching was over, everyone left, and the pandit said to me, "What brings you here? Nobody your age comes to these kinds of places, especially not of their own will – not Indian kids these days!" He laughed as he said this. I said, "Well, I was curious about this place. I've driven by many times, and I feel good being here." Pandit nodded his head as if to say, "Okay, that's good." Next he invited me upstairs to his home to have tea with him. I was very honoured by the offer. "Yes, sure, I would love to join you in your home."

So we sat upstairs and chatted about life. He told me I was a very different kind of gal – well, that was obvious considering not too many people my age really showed up at spiritual places on their own. Canadian-Indian young adults did not usually pop into a preaching and be fully engrossed in it the way I was. So he told me I was different. We also talked about yoga and meditation. I didn't know much about it back then, so he gave me a book to read. I thought it was written by him, so I humbly took it home and read it – not a big read but an easy read. I fully enjoyed it and was excited about our next encounter. I showed up quite often after that, and we would just hang out and talk about life. At one of these meetings, he told me I would be globally known. I didn't know how to handle such a strong, confident statement about myself. For a second, I felt good hearing it, but even more than that, I felt confused and lower than ever. I could not understand where it was coming from. How could he see this in me? Because honestly, I was quite a wreck. There was a sadness in me about not knowing what I was doing in life, about having no direction, no guides, no friends, no income. I had nothing, really, so how could he see the world knowing about me? And he would say it again and again. It was like he was trying to build some kind of confidence in me, but really, I didn't even know where to pull this confidence from, because I really had nothing. I never even asked him: "How or where do you see this coming from?" because I knew he was a very spiritual being. He could probably speak to the angelic realm like I do today, but at that time I didn't know about being able to speak to higher realms, though I knew he obviously had some kind of inner power and insight, so that he could see something in me that I could not even imagine about myself.

I didn't go back there for a while. I had to absorb what the pandit had said to me. Plus, life was starting to get busy. I was getting into my acting career, so I would drive from Markham to Mississauga to the Bollywood school, and when I wasn't travelling all that distance, I was rehearsing pages and pages of dialogues and monologues from scripts. My family and I had been living in a dark, small basement suite for quite some time before we found a proper home to move into. So I would spend hours and hours in the car studying scripts, and I would prepare all my material in there as I rehearsed my roles. There was no space to do that in the basement suite. There was no bedroom. We all slept in one room, which was also where the kitchen was. Luckily, it was just the three of us – my parents and me. Such a tough time it was! Such tight, small quarters, considering we had always lived in a proper, decent-sized home. It felt like we'd ended up on the curb. But I never let on to anybody about my living conditions, especially not at my acting school. I remained professional and kept my personal matters to myself. Where I was living or how I was living nobody knew. I had to be up late in my car doing dialogues in the middle of the night because that was the only quiet time I had to practice. While the world was sleeping, I was studying in the car. Finally, my family and I got ready to move to a real home, so life was rolling forward a bit now. Eventually, we moved to another area, Brampton, so I wouldn't be seeing the pandit anymore. I did try to see him before we moved – I felt a real urgency to see him – but then I heard he'd passed on. I was saddened, but I always kept his ever so confident, outlandish statement about me in my heart.

After that, my next spiritual encounter was with a guide in Rishikesh, India. By this time, I was already a practicing yogi, so from the time of my encounter with the pandit in Markham until now, many years had gone by. My time in Rishikesh with this guru was especially for doing meditation practice on the chakras. Our connection was more of an exchange. We learned from each other, and we practiced with each other. This was where my kundalini awakened, in India, with the guidance of this yogi.

After that, there were various other guides, mentors, and astrologers that I just happened to know and that would tell me some very interesting details about my present and future life. One of my family friends is an astrologer who told me six years ago that I would travel. I did not really know what he meant at the time – I thought he meant global travel. But now I know what he meant. When we met six years later, he knew I had been travelling astrally. He could recognize it in me.

I feel blessed with the many guides, both spiritual and non-spiritual, who have entered my life. I learned something from all of them. Some of the things I learned were not what I expected, but that, too, can be insightful. Some mentors will not be your ideal mentors, and things are not as they seem most of the time, but what you learn from them is still quite insightful.

Superwoman

When I was twenty-four, I was living in Vancouver with my family in our big, lovely two-story home. One day, I was home alone and bored. I needed something to do. I like to rearrange the furniture from time to time. I get bored with the same arrangement for too long, and I thought the upstairs living room area could use a new look. So I thought, "Let's move some furniture around." Our house had a basement level and a main level, and there were lots of steps leading up to the main level. Somehow I managed to pick up the full-sized heavy leather couch and get it up to the main level all by myself. I remember it was this awkward, heavy, monstrous thing, but I got it to the main level. I struggled with a lot of tight turns, and at the time I didn't realize what a majorly hazardous situation I'd got myself into. I had a lot of scares, too, while I was trying to get it completely upright. I grunted and groaned with all my might. "Come on, superwoman, lift! Push! Pull! Move it! Hold it up! Don't let it fall on your head! Come on – arms!" This was the biggest physical strength challenge I'd ever had. There were so many obstacles I didn't see coming. What if I couldn't manage to pull and lift it up or even just hold it up? What if I just couldn't? What if my arms gave out on me? It was so awkward getting around this big thing. I had to squeeze in behind the wall and climb over, one leg at a time, to get to the other side and pull it up the second flight of steps after a tight turn. And while I was trying to maneuver myself around the couch, I kept telling myself, "Don't drop the sofa!" I was afraid I was gonna slip down the stairs with this big couch falling on top of me. I'm only like 5'2", and the couch is six feet!

My hands became really sweaty as I struggled to get a grip on this massive thing. I was sweating bullets. And to make things worse, it was leather. There was no soft material to grab onto anywhere. There were many times when I felt defeated. I was scared, but I still kept that superwoman attitude alive! I had to. I had to get this thing upstairs. There it was, standing vertically in the middle of the stairs. "Come on, superwoman, it's not that heavy." Finally, I managed to get it up to the main level. Yay!! I did it! My parents came home shortly after that and saw the new arrangement in the living room. "Oh, that's nice. You brought that up? You brought the sofa upstairs?" "Yeah, I did. I brought it up by myself." I smiled. "Yup. No sweat. I just used my mighty strength." They just nodded their heads in amazement, but they were confused.

TORONTO

Sometimes I look back on my life and think, "How did I get here?" I went from being a phone sex operator to a spiritual mentor. Well, it wasn't really that easy a transition. There were plenty of hiccups – lots of odd jobs – along the way. At the time, I was new to Toronto. I had no work and no income, so I figured I'd look into an easy job so I could get some hours and get paid. I didn't actually know I was being interviewed for a position as a phone sex operator. Well, that blew my mind, to say the least. When I first went there, I thought it was like any other call centre. You call up random phone numbers and bug them to purchase air duct cleaning. So I said to myself, "What the hell? I can do this." It was a test for me to get over any shyness or social skill issues I had. So I played it cool with the cute little European manager. She was the cutest little thing I'd ever seen – so unassuming for a sex call centre. She was not your hour-glass-figure, knock-you-off-your-chair hot type. She was full-figured and cute with this great messy blonde hair, flawless skin and a distinct European accent. I looked at her pretty blue eyes and said, "Sure, I'll take the position. When do I start?"

And the great thing was nobody ever knew where I worked. All I had to say if anyone ever asked me was: "I work at a call centre." I would say it without even blinking an eye. The only time I was afraid was when I was going in and out of the building. What if I saw somebody I knew? My aunts, uncles and cousins all lived in the area. But it never happened. Who cares now, anyhow? Today I can share the experience, but at the time I was like a hawk, watching all around me.

When I think back on those times, I remember it was one of those very odd jobs that happened along the way to finding myself. I was struggling to earn an income, and this was an easy way to make a quick buck if you weren't shy. The problem was I *was* shy, so I just had to get over it and do what needed to be done. I figured what better way to overcome shyness than by making all kinds of sex sounds so the whole call centre could hear you?

I actually quite enjoyed being an operator. It was a pretty fun, entertaining job. We had a lot of good laughs there. You cannot work in a place like that and not laugh. So I was doing a good job keeping my HDL-boosting happy hormones fit. The job profile consisted of making sex sounds for the whole four-hour shift. All us girls had our own lil' private cubicles. Well, they weren't that private. Everyone in the whole place could hear you moaning and groaning. So when we'd get off the phone, we'd have a nice lil' chuckle amongst all of us. We would make fun of the guys calling in. Men can be so silly.

My yoga path started in India in 2003. I stayed there for two years to become a Bollywood actress. However, my life's path soon changed from acting to spirituality. A couple of years before I left for Mumbai or even knew I was going to Mumbai someday, I was peacefully sitting in my family room when an unusual thing happened. A movement on the floor caught my eye, so I turned to look, and I saw a little mouse standing on its hind legs. Its ears were cocked, and it looked directly at me for a few seconds, almost like it was saying, "Hello! I will stay here for a few seconds so that you notice me." And did I ever notice it! It was the cutest little mouse I'd ever seen. It seemed almost unreal, like an animation or something, but it was there. As I fixed my eyes on it, it suddenly disappeared – just like that, with no warning. I will never forget that moment.

I told my parents about it, and they thought I was crazy. So I just let it go and decided that maybe it was my brother sending a message to the Omnipresent to present itself to me in this form – letting me know that I was surrounded by prana, by the life force of the Divine, and that my deepest thoughts were being heard.

My brother was a very spiritual person, and he acknowledged that he was not just a human form but a spiritual being. I remember when we lived in Winnipeg, Canada, that he accidentally burnt the house down – well, not the whole house but the whole garage. At the time, there was a little red Bible in it. It was his, and he read from it – and it didn't burn. Everything else in the garage was gone, burnt to a crisp, except that little red Bible. I still have it today in my prayer shrine at home. It has burnt tips on a few of its pages, but other than that, it is in top condition. It was not affected by the fire at all.

My brother Neil was perhaps more spiritual than I am while he was in his physical form. But now he's gone to the astral world and is doing very well up there and beyond. We're still very connected and always will be. Before he died, he did and said a lot of good things and purified his body, cleansing it by exercise and vegetarianism. He told me that he was going to a better place to help the people here on earth. I asked him, "How and where are you going?" He said, "I have to go to Iraq-Iran, where there is a lot of war and destruction, to help rebuild the city there and to help people." I was totally confused by my brother's statement, but at the same time I wanted to wish him well and thought he was doing a good thing. Being sixteen, I kept pestering him with questions: "When are you going, for how long, and when will you be back?" He said, "I'm not coming back. I have to go forever." I got chills and thought, "Something isn't right here." So I said, "What do you mean? You have to come back." He very nicely explained, "No, I can't come back. A lot of people need me. They need my help, and I have to help them." There was a beautiful silence, so I just let it be, but in my soul I knew something was up.

A couple of weeks later, my brother passed away – he crossed over. I knew he was going, and he wanted me to know, too. It was almost like he was preparing me for what was to come. He did his dharma before he left me, fulfilling all his brotherly duties. He taught me how to drive in the cold, icy Winterpeg snow of Winnipeg. We called it "Winterpeg" because it was so cold there. I was going too fast on the icy patches, so he told me many times, "Slow down, slow down." He was so calm with his words, but I didn't listen and smashed into some people's front yard. Oh well, at least, I didn't drive the car right into the house. Neil was so calm and collected. He even saw humour in my accident – I've never seen him so calm. Of course, he called my father, and he flipped out, but my brother was as calm as could be, like nothing really happened. It was a huge accident. We were there for the next five hours, out in the cold, deep snow, waiting for the tow truck to come and pull my car out.

It all makes sense to me now that he was so calm and always playing the father role, teaching me the right way to do things. He taught me how to check the oil, and he also taught me a neat little trick to start the engine when it's acting up because of the cold. You take a pencil and stick it in some socket thingy, and there you go – the car starts up. I was amazed at the cool stuff I was learning. My brother had reached the stage of samadhi. He was a true yogi, so that's the side he was showing me before he left his physical form.

At that time the movie *Ghost* was quite popular, and he really wanted me to sit down and watch it with him. He said, "You have to sit down and watch this whole movie with me. You can't keep getting up. You'll miss the story line." He knew I had a habit of moving around – I couldn't sit still. I sighed, "Huh, okay, if you really want me to watch it with you, fine. I'll sit and watch." So there we were watching the film *Ghost* together. In my head, I was thinking: "How is this relevant to me and him? What is the message he wants me to get out of this film?" And there it was – the scene where Patrick Swayze starts moving things around. Even though he was not in a physical form, he wanted the love of his life to know that he was still with her. His physical form may not have been present, but he was still there with her, and to prove that, he would throw and move things to let her know he was around.

Four or five days after Neil's passing, I was sitting alone on the floor in my room, leaning my back against the door, just thinking about him, when all of a sudden his baseball hat fell off the hook and into my lap. It gave me chills – but good chills. Right away, bang! – the movie *Ghost* came to mind. I smiled to myself and thought, "Really … really." Because I'm a practical person, I turned around and looked at the hook the baseball cap had been sitting on to make sure the hook was not falling off or that something else wasn't going on that would have made the cap fall into my lap. I put the cap back on the hook. How could this happen? Nothing … I got nothing – there was no logic to it. All I could see was my brother and why he needed me to sit down and watch the film *Ghost*.

It happened again a few days later. Again I was sitting in my room on the floor, just hanging out, when a framed picture of my friends and me fell right in front of me. This time it startled me because I had not been thinking about Neil. But I wasn't scared. I actually got a feeling of comfort, security and protection – that was the message he wanted to give me. More and more, I knew that he was always with me, even though he was not in a physical form. But again I was trying to figure out the logic of how it could happen, and again I got no answer other than that he was doing it all and that he was with me.

The framed picture was quite heavy and had been sitting in the middle of my record player. Yes, at that time, we still had record players, although this one had a built-in cassette player, too. So there really was no logic for how it could have leaped up off the player and ended up in front of me, especially with the frame being as heavy as it was. My thought to myself was that it must have taken a lot of energy out of Neil to do that, but he did it for me. Neil protects me, like the older brother and father figure that he was. When things in my life are grey and I can't figure them out, I feel that Neil is with me, giving me his take on things. He also sends me messages in my sleep.

This next story took place at a time when I didn't really know where I was going in life. It was back at the time I was training for Bollywood, doing an acting course in Mississauga, in Ontario. I took the course very seriously. I had always envisioned a bright acting future unfolding for me some day. I could see the limelight and the big dream, but there was still a bit of hesitation and confusion in my head. Finally I settled it all, and two years later I decided to move to Mumbai. I had the support of one of my friends, who said, "Sure, come on down. I'll get you a good role in a film I'm producing, a big film that's coming up." On the strength of that promise, without blinking an eye, I got on a plane and flew to Mumbai. I didn't get the role. I don't think there actually was one for me. That's a whole other story, but now that I was in Mumbai, he thought, "What should I do about the fake promises I gave her?" He got his secretary to take me around the town and show me some of the sights and the shopping area. She took me to a major Ganesh Temple called Shree Siddhivinayak Ganapati Temple. She was eager for me to be blessed there. I didn't mind – I was open to it, so we got a tray to give as a devotional offering. I decorated it with some flowers and fruit and some money that I was donating, and we stood in line and waited our turn to be blessed by the temple priest. As we approached the priest, we saw a huge statue of a mouse, with a little mouse sitting on top of the huge mouse. My secretary friend told me to whisper in the ear of the big mouse. I said, "What?" With a nice big smile and a slight chuckle, she repeated, "Yeah, I mean it … Do it. Whisper your wish in its ear." Then it clicked: "OMG! It's the little mouse I saw standing in my house on its hind legs, the one that perked up its ears, stared at me and then disappeared." This was the same mouse – that was the connection. So my eyes lit up, and I told it my wish. I felt a bit stupid whispering into the ear of this mouse statue, but I obviously did it.

So that was why the Omnipotent came to me in the form of a mouse once again – to let me know that It was there with me. It showed this to me in a weird way the time, but I guess It needed to add some comic relief to my life. I needed it, and It knew I could use something cute and fun. It boosted my mood and gave me encouragement. It validated the thoughts I was having about my life. I felt at peace.

INDIA AND BOLLYWOOD

This all took place before I found my spiritual path. I was in India as an aspiring actress, and ironically, it was in Mumbai, the city of big dreams, that I was connecting spiritually.

Because I was living in India, my life was full of strange and unconventional things, like having to use a bucket full of water to flush the toilet. In India the plumbing doesn't function the way it does with Western toilets. Indian toilets get easily clogged, so you have to manually flush the waste. Not nice. It works the same way as Western outhouses do. I also had to get creative, finding ways to go to the bathroom for a week, because I had no toilet. Wow, that was challenging! That's what I call roughing it. It was like camping. I had no toilet. They dug out a space for me so I could get a commode installed in place of an Indian toilet, which is more or less a hole in the ground that you squat over to do your thing.

Once, I had to sleep in a friend's office for a week. I had no home, so he let me sleep on the couch in his office. I'll never forget those tough days. Thinking of them brings me back to 2001, when I purposely trained myself to sleep surrounded by many, many objects cluttering my bed. It looked like the space had been hit by a tornado and everything had landed right on my bed. People would have thought I was crazy to sleep with all that stuff on my bed, but I knew that someday I would have to sleep in cramped, uncomfortable quarters, and now I was fully prepared.

I remember getting my first apartment and being happy with it from the get-go. I had a friend take me around and show me different apartments. I said to myself: "I am not going to waste time. If I like the first place I see, I will make it my home." And that's exactly what I did.

It was a nice flat in the Lokhandwala Complex, the main residential area for Bollywood. I cleaned it for three days straight. Scrubbed every nook and cranny of the floors and made it home. On my third day in the place, I started to notice some perfectly round purple dots of some sort of liquid on the floor – just a few spots here and there. I didn't think much of the incident, but it did capture my attention. I knew I hadn't dropped anything, because I had just finished cleaning the floor so it was spic and span. And I hadn't eaten anything of a deep purple colour, so I shrugged the whole thing off and just took a cloth and wiped the floor.

The next day, I saw the same deep purple spots on the floor again. And again, they were perfectly round. Now they definitely caught my attention. This time I rubbed my finger across them, sniffing as I tried to determine what they might be, but I got nothing – they were odorless. The whole thing was unusual. I got the cloth and wiped them up again. The following day, I actually went looking for them, but when I came home, there was nothing there.

Then, on the fourth day after I first saw them, they were there again – the same spots. Now I was freaking. For a moment, I thought, "Could it be my brother? Could it be Neil sending me a message, letting me know he's here with me, that I'm not alone in India?" So I wiped them up again. Then I sat down to calm myself by reading one of my books, a Sufi book of poems and quotes. When I opened the book, it opened right up to a page with a purple flower! I was completely shocked and ecstatic at the same time! I thought: "What is this phenomenon that's happening to me?" I called my friend and told him, and then I called my mum and told her, too. My mum told me, "Don't worry. It's your brother blessing you, because it's Rakhi these days, and he wants you to know he's there with you. All other brothers and sisters in India are celebrating Rakhi, so he is celebrating it with you, too." Hearing that from her made me feel really peaceful and special in a way that words cannot explain.

Another unusual incident that happened to me in Mumbai had to do with a little yellow book that I had. It had a frog on the cover, and I would write all my notes in it. One evening, as I got to the main gate of the apartment complex, I happened to look down at the ground to my left, and I saw a frog just sitting there, staring up at me. So I stared back at it with the same intensity. It wouldn't move. The next thing I knew, it disappeared – poof! – into thin air. I stared intensely at the spot, thinking, "Where did it go?" Then I just chuckled to myself, accepted it, and smiled as I thought, "Okay, I get it. It's because I write all my important things in this little yellow frog book of mine. This frog was letting me know that whatever I was doing was right on." It was the only sense I could make of this unusual encounter with my little frog friend. Now that I'm accustomed to it, all this spiritual stuff has become the norm, but back then I was still getting used to it.

I remember, when I was about 27 years old, I bought a sunset topaz stone. I wanted to wear a necklace that represented me, and sunset topaz was my birthstone. I really gravitated towards it when I saw it in the jewelry shop. It was such a deep orange, just like its name, "sunset topaz". I put it on a nice chain and wore it day and night. I never took it off. After a few days of wearing it, I noticed that when I woke up in the morning, the stone had left an imprint on my chest.

At first I tried to figure out the science of how this happened, so I thought, "Oh, it probably pressed deep against my skin while I was sleeping and left its imprint." But then I stared carefully at the mark on my chest, and I knew that it hadn't pressed deeply against my skin, because that would have faded away after a few hours. It was as though someone had taken a perfect holographic image of the stone and placed it on my chest. I was truly amazed – I felt like a kid with cotton candy.

I remember going to a restaurant-lounge on my own that evening to celebrate by myself. I sat next to a stranger at the bar, and as I was having a drink, he asked me, "What brings you here on your own?" I was at a slight loss for words, thinking, "Well, how can I tell him what just happened to me? If I say it out loud, it's going to lose its value, and he's gonna think I'm cuckoo. But I went for it, anyhow. I told him about my stone experience and how I believed it was a blessing. To me, as I was soul searching and looking for something to guide me, I felt I'd received this special message from above. I think I lost him somewhere along the way. Alcohol will do that. You're not as coherent in a bar, and on top of that, it's loud and you tend to talk about everything but spirituality. He did take a close look, though. He held my necklace gently in his hands and looked at the mark on my chest. It looked faded, partly because it was so dark in there and partly because it was quite late at night, and the beauty of the hologram stone image was starting to disappear. It had stayed with me all day long and pretty much all evening. Now that I think about it, perhaps it was disappearing on me because I was in a bar having a drink, which was insulting the precious stone's vibrations. That message in itself prompted me to make my way out. I left the friendly stranger with a warm good-bye.

I wore that sunset topaz for a few years. It stayed on me the whole time I lived in Mumbai – I never took it off. That little stone held a miraculous power that only I knew about. It looked unassuming to others, so it suited my time in Mumbai perfectly. And it looked nice on my neck, very delicate and subtle. I wore it on a black thread. It was quite a stunning colour, and even though it was small and subtle, you couldn't help but notice it. The deep sunset orange and the black thread complemented each other nicely.

In fact, I remember it got in the way of making love with someone I adored and was completely in awe of. Let's call him Mr. Composed. That's what he was – always composed, untroubled and serene in every situation. That stone gave me such great ethereal energy. It transmitted it to me like nobody's business. In the same way, the love between Mr. Composed and me was the intense energy of two kindred spirits who were meant to share. It was so powerful that few words ever needed to be exchanged. It was a silent love affair. Its beauty lay in its silence, just like the silence that spoke through my beautiful sunset topaz.

Certain scents evoke nostalgic memories, and for me, it was like that with that precious stone. I understand now that the person I wanted then I couldn't have. My life experiences at that time and my choice to become an actress were not something he could agree with. I was driven by a full-force intensity to become an actress. Nobody could stop me. Whether I became one or not, I sure wasn't going to give up trying. He knew that, so our chapter came to an end. I didn't make too much of a fuss when he wanted to end things. I knew why it was happening, but I knew that the reason I had come to Mumbai was to become an actress, not to get caught up in a love affair, so I stuck to my guns and maintained my discipline to do what I had set out to do there.

So when Mr. Composed spoke his mind about ending things, I didn't say much. In chivalrous fashion, he kindly showed me to the door of his flat. As he shut the door, I grabbed the stone tightly, as if I were holding onto it for dear life and speaking to it in my own way. Suddenly, he reopened the door. I wasn't expecting that, and he caught me holding onto the stone. He looked at me in shock as if he realized in that very moment how precious our relationship was to me and how affected I had been by this sudden ending. He saw that grabbing the stone was giving me some kind of solace. At least he knew then that he was pretty important to me and that the stone was important enough that it, too, held significance. Every time we'd made love, the stone had always been right there, catching his eye with its dangling and swinging.

I struggled during my acting days in Mumbai, running from one producer to the next, meeting with different "camps", as they call them. I got this one gig for a modelling shoot. I wasn't exactly thrilled with the gig, but I accepted the job because I needed the cash. I really didn't care for modelling. It wasn't as meaty as acting for me, and I only took the gig out of desperation.

The modelling gig was miles away from Mumbai in a town close to Shirdi. The town of Shirdi itself was famous for Sai Baba, a great enlightened soul who walked the earth around the late 1800s. He was highly regarded as a fakir, guru, and yogi. He was well loved because of his unconventional way of preaching – young and old all loved him. Today he is still highly regarded all over India, especially by the Bollywood film industry. At the time, though, I knew little about Shirdi and nothing at all about Sai Baba.

So there I was on the bus on my way to a small town near Shirdi to do a modelling shoot for a five-star hotel. The journey was long. We travelled from the time it was light till far into the night. It took nearly an entire day. It was really hard to hear the bus conductor announcing the stops, so I purposely sat beside a lady who looked trustworthy enough that I felt comfortable asking her to please tell me when my stop came up. She said, "No problem. I will let you know. But you have a long way to go. Shirdi is the last stop on the journey, and your stop is a couple before Shirdi." I felt relieved, and as I was sleep-deprived from all the travelling I had been doing, I sat back, relaxed and closed my eyes.

After what seemed like forever, the bus finally arrived at the last stop and everybody started to get off. I was confused. I wasn't sure if this was my stop, because the lady had said that my town was almost the last stop – but this *was* the last stop. I asked her if this was the stop where I needed to get off for my town. She said, "No, you missed it. It was a few stops back. You're in Shirdi now!" "Oh, my God," I sighed. I didn't get angry with her, though. What would I say to her? What was done was done. She'd probably dozed off. Anyhow, there I was in Shirdi, panicked about what to do now because it was already four in the morning. The other passengers getting off the bus all suggested that I stay there at the Hotel Neeta International for the night since it was too late to get a taxi, and it wasn't safe to try.

I was unsure of what to do. I had very little money – not even enough for a hotel room. I stepped into the lobby and explained to the owner the importance of the modeling gig the next day. I rambled on about how I was supposed to be in another town a few miles back but had missed my stop. "I'm not supposed to be here. I have a modeling job tomorrow." The hotel owner listened patiently to my rambling with an encouraging smile. "Don't you worry," he said. "You are where you need to be. You are in exactly the right place." I tried to argue, showing him my paper directions. "No, you don't understand. I'm not supposed to be in Shirdi." He continued to smile. "Yes, you are my dear. You have been called by Shirdi Sai

Baba. You are very a blessed person. Sai does not call everyone to his quarters." I was not amused by his smile or his calm attitude. He kept repeating his statement about being called by Sai Baba, but I was too much of a wreck to hear what he was saying. I had no idea who Sai Baba was, and I was not impressed by the owner's persistence. "I could care less about Sai Baba or why you think he's calling me," I said. Little did I know then the power of a patient man and a holy saint.

Eventually, my emotions calmed down a little. The hotel owner convinced me to spend the night at the hotel, where I slept on a couch in the lobby to save money. He had been calm from the get-go, and now he repeated to me, "Dear, stay here for the night. Then go in the morning to Sai Baba to do your darshan, and everything will be fine. After that, you can make your way to the town where you need to do your modelling shoot." I said, "Okay, what do I need to do for darshan?" He said, "Buy a thali for 100-200 rupees, whatever you can afford. And on that thali, put a coconut, some fruit and a red cloth. I said, "Where do I go from the hotel? How far do I have to walk?" I was still in a state of disarray. He explained, "Not far at all. You will see little stands where you can purchase the thali all along the path up to the temple. Then make your way to the temple. Get in the queue, and do your darshan to Sai Baba when you see the figure. And that's it," he said with a smile.

I made my way to the thali store, where I watched as the other people offered 3000 to 5000 rupees, the equivalent of 50 to 100 dollars. Many of them had traveled miles and saved for months to do their darshan. I, the "Westerner", as I was often called, had less than ten dollars in my pockets, and I was instructed to split that between the thali and the temple fees. I was nervous when I reached the merchant. "How much?" I asked. He advised me to give whatever I liked. Ashamed, I offered him 200 rupees, less than three US dollars. To my surprise, he gladly accepted it and handed me a beautiful thali.

So there I was in line, holding my thali with nearly a thousand people ahead of me and behind me. I was not expecting such a huge crowd. The massive statue of Sai Baba sat before me. It was so pleasantly serene, the opposite of my life at that moment. Suddenly, an electrical vibration swept beneath my feet and passed over my entire body. I began to weep uncontrollably. At the time, I did not understand my tears, but I now know that the power of the energy I was receiving from Shirdi Sai Baba's teachings were real. The statue was no longer a mere statue, but a manifestation of Sai Baba's love and blessings. The hotel owner had been right. I had been called by Sai Baba. He was saying, "I've called you here, and you have come. Welcome!" I was humbled in a way I had never felt before. I whispered an inner prayer. "Yes, Sai Baba, I am here. Please help me. Be with me." The words of the owner floated back into my head: *You are a very blessed person. Sai doesn't call everyone to his quarters, but he has called you. This is why you missed your stop – to be here with him at Shirdi!*

From that moment, I felt elated. I felt like nothing would go wrong now. As I got on the bus the next morning to go to the shoot, just as the bus was about to take off and the tires were already rolling, someone started banging on the door. The bus conductor stopped to let him in. It was my friend, the hotel owner. He was huffing and puffing, and he came right up to my seat. In his hand, he held a framed picture of Sai Baba to give to me. He said, "I needed to give you this before you went, so that your journey would be safe and you would get all good things in life and be successful on your life path." I smiled at him with deep emotion and thanked him for taking such strong actions to get this framed Sai Baba picture to me. I would go to my shoot and from then on, all good things would happen. Anyhow, to make a long story short, the shoot didn't happen, but now I understand that it was for the best. The vibrations from the people organizing the shoot were not good, so it was not meant to be. I understood that Sai was keeping me safe from harm.

Staying In Juhu And The Bhagavad Gita

I bought my first Bhagavad Gita ever in Mumbai, India. I was staying as a paying guest in Juhu. Juhu is an affluent residential area of Mumbai for many Bollywood celebrities. The flat I stayed in had a beautiful tenth-floor view overlooking the famous Juhu beach on the Arabian Sea. Although I was a paying guest, it felt more like a family environment, which was quite comforting for me, considering I was alone in a big city with lots of lights and a lot of chaos. A friend of mine, who is a big shot in the Mumbai film industry, managed a lot of A-list celebs, and he got me in touch with the landlords. He felt it would be a suitable environment for me, since I was a gal from Canada looking to be an actress in Mumbai, and this place had "actor" written all over it. There was even an actress in the family, who had been famous back in the day. She didn't live there because it was her sister's home, but she did sleep over sometimes. In fact, my room was her room.

The flat was right in the middle of Celebrity Central. Because my friend was the manager for some of the A-list Bollywood stars, I even had the privilege of having dinner with one of them at my friend's flat in Juhu. My own room at the flat I was renting was a closet-sized space, but I made the best of it. My diction teacher once said to me, "You live in such a small space, but you have done a nice job making it into a living space to call a temporary home." I smiled and said, "Yes, that's right. I don't mind – it's my nice little sanctuary." Again, I have to give credit to the training I gave myself by sleeping on a tornado-strewn bed in 2001.

I got good vibes for my acting career from my little 8x8-foot room. Yes, it was tiny, but I loved it – I didn't need a lot. The place was modern, and my landlords were hip. I absolutely fell in love with the place and the people. It was a done deal. Here I was in Juhu, Mumbai, ready to start my acting career, and the people I was staying with were so wonderful. I loved every moment of being there. In the evenings, we would get together and just sit outside on the balcony and look out towards the Arabian Sea. With the cool breeze hitting my face, I would peacefully collect my thoughts. I spent a lot of time out there on my own, too. It was heaven. My diction master would come and give me Hindi and Urdu lessons to correct my tone, pronunciation, etc. He and I would spend our lessons studying out on the balcony – we enjoyed it so much. I love nature, and this was the closest I got to it in a big city like Mumbai.

In the daytime, I would spend my days wandering about the town exploring things, seeing how people lived, going to various restaurants. And then I discovered the Hare Rama Hare Krishna temple in Juhu. Wow! I was so thrilled! I was like a kid in a candy store. I spent so much time there I practically made it my second home. It was so convenient, too. From where I was staying, it was just a quick five-minute rickshaw ride to the temple. Well, in Mumbai's traffic, it ended up taking longer, but it was close to my home, anyhow. I would just wander around, appreciating the beauty of the temple and all the Hare Rama Hare Krishna yogis in their orange robes. Sometimes I would go into the main hall and listen to the chanting, or I would wander on the outskirts of the temple, enjoying the flowers and the people sitting on the steps, just hanging out and taking in the good vibrations of the energies floating in the air.

At one point, I came across a bookstand that had many, many copies of the Bhagavad Gita for sale for 100 rupees. I debated whether to buy one or not. I did not know a lot about the Bhagavad Gita, and it looked so thick. I thought to myself, "Am I really going to read this?" But then the bookseller encouraged me, of course. He would – that was his job. He kept saying, "Take, take … only 100 rupees, just 100 rupees – take, take!" So what to do? I got excited, and because I was a good sport, I said, "Okay, give me one!" The second he handed it to me and it was in my hands, I hugged it tightly against my chest as if to say, "This is mine. It's my book!" I felt really good, like all of a sudden there was hope, an inner joy. I felt like my life had meaning and purpose. I was excited to go home and read it. And it made me feel smart, too. I was proud to have this big, thick book that I hugged in my arms. What an empowering book! Without even opening a page of it, that was the effect the Bhagavad Gita had on me.

During that time, I took lessons in a form of Indian dance called Kathak. My dance teacher was also a Christian preacher in the evenings. I would go to her home in the daytime to do my dance lessons, and as our relationship grew, she invited me one day to join her Bible teachings on Sundays. I think she must have known I could have used some soulful love. I was very grateful to be invited but a little nervous about going. I didn't know much about Christianity. And I had never been to any Bible readings before. I had no idea what to expect of a Bible reading, and I conjured up a bunch of "what ifs" in my head. What if they asked me to stand up and comment on the Bible? What if I got put on the spot like that? What if I ended up saying something really dumb that's not even in the Bible but in the Quran or something? OMG, I might start a riot. Everyone will be shouting at me. Their arms will be flapping everywhere, and their faces will be red with anger. No, I couldn't go. I tried to politely decline. "Oh, I'm not sure. I don't know." I wasn't sure if it was the right place for me to be. I didn't want to insult anyone's beliefs or, even worse, make a fool of myself. My dance teacher was so polite: "You must come. It will be a real pleasure to have you join us. Please come. I will introduce you to everyone." I decided I would go.

Sunday evening arrived. I wore my best church outfit, a long frock-type dress. I was so nervous just walking up to the house. I could hear all the people chatting through the window. I stopped to listen for a few minutes to get a feel for what was going on inside. It sounded like everyone was having a good time, laughing and enjoying themselves. It didn't sound serious and quiet, like I expected it to. It almost sounded more like a party than a Bible reading. But what did I know? Maybe this was how things went at Bible readings. I entered, and my dance teacher greeted me with a big hug and a smile. "Come, sit." She introduced me to this person and that person. I thought, "Wow, this is a breeze, I could have walked in a long time ago. Not much Bible talk going on here." But then the real stuff started. Everyone quieted down, and they all took a seat on a chair or the floor. I sat on the floor. My teacher laid down some floor sheets for everyone's comfort. In India, the homes are tight, small spaces. People all have to cram in.

And then it began. They all pulled out their Bible, *The Message of Love, the New Testament*. I'm not sure if this was the Bible or a smaller scripture, like verses from the Bible. But it had familiar passages that I'd heard here and there. Everyone opened up to the discussion chapter for the evening. I didn't have a book, so I just listened. I remember one middle-aged gentleman started the reading in English. He spoke English well. His voice was clear and crisp. I can't remember now what the chapter or topic of discussion was, but I remember the feeling. I felt good. I felt really good. I felt so welcomed – everyone greeted me so nicely. There I was, in the midst of all these strangers all around me, listening to the words of God. I sat there holding my knees tucked to my chest, just immersed in the whole experience, trying not to miss each beautiful verse or line. I was like a kid intensely listening to a bedtime story. I just absolutely fell in love with everything I was hearing. A lot of it didn't totally make sense to me, yet somehow it did.

Credit I suppose also goes to the gentlemen who was explaining the verses from the Bible so cheerfully and charismatically. I went back for a few more Sundays. I dedicated my Sundays to these Bible reading get-togethers. My dance teacher gifted me the same holy book, *The Message of Love, the New Testament.* She signed it, too: "With Love & Blessings From Hindi Care Cell." I don't know what Care Cell is. I suppose that's maybe the name of the group that got together.

What amazed me was that I was a gal from Canada who knew nothing about Christianity. India taught me Christianity. I had lived in North America all my life and grown up with Christian friends, yet I learnt more about Jesus and the Bible in India. I never would have guessed it – my newfound knowledge of Jesus would be learnt in India, of all places. I never knew how many Christians lived in India until I was actually living there myself. The people belonging to the Christian group I met with were all Indian Christians. I assumed Indians living in India would mostly be Hindu. I was definitely wrong about that.

Now that I had this holy book in my hands, I had to read it. I was very excited. I would save it for the very last thing I did in my day. In the daytime, I was all over Mumbai, and when I finally got back home to my flat in the evening, before going to bed, I would pick up my little holy book and read away. I got so much insight and inspiration from it. It allowed me to keep going and keep doing what I needed to do in this bloodsucking city of Mumbai. I read and read each night. It was November now, my birth month. I was twenty-nine, and my thirtieth birthday was coming up soon. I made a promise to myself that I would finish this holy book before my thirtieth birthday. I still had so many pages to go. I read and read each night. I read until my eyes were heavy. But even with heavy eyes, I got an extra pump of energy – from where, I don't know. Every now and then, the holy book gave me something to keep going. Something I read would give me a lift to read a few more pages. Finally, it was the eve of my birthday. I remember I still had a lot of pages to complete before the clock struck twelve. It was so close. It was 11:30 p.m. OMG, was I gonna make it? Read, read! Yay!! I finally finished the holy book! I finished at like 11:45. I felt so overjoyed! Words can't explain it enough. I felt so complete because I completed The New Testament on time. The book gave me so much …

The lights were completely off, and it was totally dark in my flat. I lived on the tenth floor. I had a big window, and many nights I would get lost in the view. The only lights shining into my flat were the street lights and the light from the night sky. I patiently waited for my birthday to arrive as I lost myself in the view. As I lay there on the comfortable mat that was my bed, I just stared up at the sky. In that moment, I asked God, "Come on, God, give me something – it's my thirtieth birthday. Give me anything. Maybe I'll see a unicorn flying through the sky." Nothing. I got nothing. I was sad, but I still had a few minutes left before the clock hit twelve. I started thinking, "Well, maybe this is it. Maybe I get just silence. No unicorns, no shooting stars. But it's my thirtieth. Come on, give me something!"

Then I noticed three very dim stars. They were really hard to see – I was squinting just to see them. The stars slowly started getting closer and brighter. They were moving closer to me, and I could see them clearly now. They were very clear, very bright. I got so excited, I was almost jumping up and down. Three! three! you're showing me three! My number and my birthday number! But then, something else happened. No way! I saw the 0 – a 3 and an 0, like in 30. The full moon was so bright I can't put it into words. I don't even know where it came from. It was just there all of a sudden. I hadn't seen it before. There had just been stars in the sky – the three stars I saw. But then the three stars and the full moon came together and lined up next to each other to say "Happy 30th" to me. They were in a really obvious line. Happy 30th!

I was blown away. I was so emotional. This was the greatest thirtieth birthday gift I could ever get. Nothing could top this – nothing. I got something that was literally out of this world. I thanked and thanked and thanked God that night. I celebrated my thirtieth with myself, the stars and the moon. We had a great time. We exchanged so many words. We just spoke to each other the whole night. I had the best birthday ever. They wanted to give me this special gift so I would know that my thirties were going to be something – a revelation of a new beginning. Everything started from that moment. Actually, the moment I picked up that holy book and started reading it, things were already changing. The stars and the moon were telling me that I was headed for a new, adventurous life. By the way, I was completely sober – no intoxication of any kind.

When I was thirty, I experienced another incident like the one in the Vancouver parking lot. At the time, I was in Mauritius doing a film shoot. Those were my Bollywood days, and I was there with the crew to do a one-month shoot. I was the second lead, and the lead actress and I were staying at a different hotel from the rest of the crew. We were separated from them for many reasons. The producers put us up at the luxury hotel, since we were the lead actors. Also, we were the only foreigners in the film, so out of respect, they gave us a nicer suite to stay in. And lastly, boys stayed with boys, and girls stayed with girls – there was that kind of thing going on.

We had fun during the film shoot – it was a good time in Mauritius. My co-star and I settled into our separate suites. We had a beautiful view looking out over the sea, with the warm winds hitting our faces and the smell of fresh air. After we settled in, we met downstairs at the main restaurant to have dinner. Then she said to me, "Hey, how about we walk over to where the boys are staying and hang out with them?" By this time, it must have been close to 10:30 p.m. I said to her, "I don't know. It's kinda late to be walking there right now." But she said, "Oh, don't worry, we'll be fine."

She managed to convince me, but I wasn't really feeling too safe. Anyhow, we made our way outside and started walking the dark streets of Mauritius. There was not a sound on the road. It was so eerie. Every step was torture because the road we were walking on was like a really long, dark back alleyway. In the daytime, the streets looked totally different. Next thing we knew, there was a wild dog chasing us. My co-actress started to run, but I said, "Don't run. Slow right down." She said, "But it looks wild – like it's going to attack." I confirmed what she was saying. "That's right. That's why you need to slow down. Don't let it think you're afraid. Make it your friend. Bring a feeling of sweetness towards it into your mind." So we slowed down, and we saw that the dog also stopped growling. We continued our smooth, steady pace and avoided turning around to look. Finally, we realized it had left. The dog was gone – whew!

So we carried on. We just wanted to get to where the boys were, but it seemed like it was taking forever. It was a good forty-minute walk, and it seemed like we were never gonna get there. Once things quieted down, we found ourselves again in a noiseless, dark alley. All of a sudden, a car appeared out of nowhere. All we could see were bright headlights behind us. We kept turning around to see where it was going, and I realized that it was following us, so I told her, "They're after us." She said, "No, they're not. They're just driving." I said "Nope – I wish. But there are no other cars on the road and no other people in sight at this late hour. They're up to no good. They're after us." Right then, the car sped up, and I said, "Run!" We ran as fast as we could until we found a small bush on someone's lawn, and we hid behind it. We scrunched down and kept so silent that not even a breath could be heard from either one of us. We stayed put as we saw the car getting closer, but the headlights were hard on our eyes. We slowly turned around in the bush, away from the road and the sight of the car so that we were facing the house. We stayed very quiet. We could hear the car's engine idling. It was waiting for us. Finally, we could see through the bush that the car started to reverse. We could breathe again. We got out of the bush and started walking towards our destination at an extremely fast pace. We weren't expecting it, but our movements caught the driver's eye again, and the car did a quick U-turn, so again we started running for our lives.

This time we were closer to our destination. We ran and ran, with the car right behind us. We started screaming, "Help, help, help!" The boys all came out onto the balcony and saw us, and they said, "What's going on?" We saw the car turn away, and we pointed at it. We were completely out of breath as we said, "That car – it was chasing us." The crew came down, welcomed us in, and we explained the whole incident with the wild dog and the car thugs. They said, "Well, you guys probably shouldn't have been walking at this time of night. This is Mauritius, and nobody walks around after 9 p.m., especially females." Well, I knew now to never do it again.

My acting career eventually turned into my yoga path, but while I was a struggling actress, I had no money and no job, and I was constantly going for interviews and auditions, hoping to land that big break. I had to travel in bumpy auto-rickshaws to get everywhere, and some of the destinations took two hours to get to. By the time I got there, I looked like a complete wreck. So much for looking like a glamour girl, which is what Bollywood is all about. There I was, with half my hair falling out because it had become so thin and frail. I looked like a hospital patient. After travelling in dust and pollution for two hours and looking like that, I was bound to not get the gig. Those were rough days.

Even when my Bollywood acting career didn't go the way I wanted it to, great things started brewing beneath it all. First, the owners of the gym where I trained in 2004 offered me a job. I had become good friends with them, and they knew I was struggling, as all actors do when they're first trying to make their way in the industry. So I was happy to take the job minding the front desk and getting people to become members.

It was a lively atmosphere to work in. The gym was pumping every evening, since that was when most of the crowd would come to do their workouts. The music was always hyped up, too.

It was like being in a club environment every evening – just what my mind needed to keep things active and happy in my head. And of course I was earning some money. It wasn't that much, but I was ever so grateful for what I was making. Even a small income went a long way in Mumbai. Still, it was an expensive city to live in, so every rupee counted. Mumbai is the hub of the Bollywood industry, and it was *the* cosmopolitan city that everyone wanted to be a part of and somehow leave their mark on, if they could. Just like New York City, it's a buzzing city with so much to offer. My friends, the owners of the gym, also offered me a position as a personal trainer to some of the girls who went there. I was thrilled! I quickly made up my mind and told them, "Yes, I can do this." That was the catalyst that brought me to my current yoga path.

There are a few important factors that cannot be ignored when explaining why the drive to do this was there. For one thing, I was in love with the owner, who was also my friend. Let's call him Mr. Calm, as that's what represents him best. He was cool, calm, and collected. My love for Mr. Calm was intense because he helped me during one of my toughest times, as my stay in Mumbai was one of the greatest challenges of my life. Mr. Calm's generosity and kindness were always silent. He never asked me, "Are you struggling? Would you like some help?" He just did what needed to be done by providing me with work. This silent gesture of kindness made my heart grow fonder of him by the minute. I didn't know anybody in the city, so I was pretty much alone in Mumbai, and when Mr. Calm gave me a hand, it meant the world to me.

So many new beginnings were arising out of this intense period of my life.

Without ever knowing it, Mr. Calm shifted my way of thinking. I was experiencing new beliefs, like the possibility that I didn't need to be an actress. I really enjoyed being in the health and fitness circle. Maybe, I thought, I could do this as a career. This thought repeatedly hammered at my mind. It was a loud voice I could not ignore, and things were looking bright with this sudden vision of a career change. I felt such a rush with my energy levels being up. Of course, this made my love for Mr. Calm grow even more. It didn't help that he was tall, dark and handsome, and his presence was so strong that when he was in the room, you couldn't miss him. When he walked into the gym, the whole energy of the place changed. Every guy wanted to be him and have his physique. He had an amazing physique. Every other guy in the place would be sweating bullets, working out three times as hard to emulate Mr. Calm's physique. He was perfectly proportioned – not too big and bulky, like an overtrained muscle-popping giant, but tall and lean with just the right cuts.

Mumbai was the greatest journey of my life and a chapter I would not erase. It's the reason I'm here today, doing what I do. As far as the juicy part of Mumbai goes, well, I don't have much, but from a distance, sure, I met some A-list stars while working at the gym. The gym was quite reputable because of its ties with Bollywood actors. The owners themselves trained the A-list stars. Every now and then, to create more hype for their gym, they would ask the celebs to pop in for a guest appearance, do a bit of training and leave. I once met one of the stars up close and personal while I was at Mr. Calm's flat. We were exiting the bedroom together. Coming out of the room together made it a slightly awkward moment, but we handled it fine. After all, I was with Mr. Calm, who knew how to handle any situation. The A-list star, of course, would not have remembered me and didn't really know who I was. He was cordial to me because I was with Mr. Calm, and I was pretty low-profile. I had no reason to be anything else, as I was just one of the many faces of Mumbai's aspiring actresses.

In the end, I can fairly say that there were just a couple of milestones that triggered my beautiful life path. Maybe, in a way, the high-energy job at the gym and my love affair with Mr. Calm, who was tall, dark and handsome with a big heart, acted like the power of persuasion. And their power worked. It all began in Mumbai, so Mumbai was the beginning of an end and also of a new chapter in my life.

BACK TO TORONTO

I guess I had the bug bad! I didn't stop with Bollywood when I got back to Canada in 2005. Not long after that, I registered with a Toronto acting agency and started the whole process all over again. Going to acting classes, learning monologues and dialogues, doing 8x10 photo shoots ... I guess I wasn't ready to give up the acting career yet. I still had some juice left in me to give Hollywood a shot. With all the skills, acting training and new experiences I'd gained from living in Bollywood for two years, how could I just give up acting?

I was determined to get myself into Hollywood, so I kept myself disciplined. I showed up eager for each acting class. I was very optimistic about life and where I was going. Finally, the day came when my acting coach told me they had made a shortlist of potential future Hollywood actors to go give it a shot in LA. Acting agencies were taking new talent right now, and this could be the big break. My fellow actors and I were ready – this was what we wanted to hear. Then my name got called: "Yup, Reyna, you're on the list. You should go to L.A and give it your best. We're supporting you from our agency here in Toronto."

That support wasn't much, though. I still had to buy the flight ticket and everything else on my own. What they did was to let us know which hotel to stay at in Beverly Hills and that we were basically representing Toronto talent. So there I was for three days in LA, staying at some Best Western Inn in Beverly Hills, going for non-stop meet-and-greets to present my monologue to top Hollywood acting agencies and management. My monologue was Shakespearean – one of Viola's scenes from *Twelfth Night*, but with a twist. I had just come back from Mumbai and Bollywood, so my English needed some polishing. My agent gave me a great idea – to put a modern spin on the monologue by making it into a black girl, hip hop "F this F that" routine. It was quite funny, actually, now that I think about it. I remember a lot of agents liked it. They all said, "Wow, that was different! We like the twist on it." One agent said, "You're like a rough, tough Angelina Jolie." She was a bit harsh, though, because she also added, "Well, if you're gonna be this image, then you'd better get some tattoos and piercings done immediately." I handled it well and said, "Sure, if that's what you think I need to do to keep up this image, I can do that." I didn't actually do it but just said, "Yes, ma'am," to be non-confrontational. She wasn't expecting me to be so positive, with such a cheerful disposition.

Anyhow, I carried on with my hip hop, black girl "F this F that" Shakespeare monologue. It was a long three days. Nothing came of it, but I had no regrets – I needed to do this. I didn't feel bad. Things just didn't work out in LA. I knew I gave it all I could and more. Who does Bollywood first for two years and then comes back to make a go of Hollywood? Looking back, I'm sometimes surprised that I had such drive and passion for acting. That time period definitely gave me my fair share of life experiences that became a part of my inner knowledge, strength, power and wisdom.

Soul

One has lots of money
The other has little money

One is studious
The other, spiritual

One drinks wine
The other, a soda please!

One is a thunderbolt
The other, calm as waves

One comes from plenty
The other is empty

But they both have soul!

The great thing was that, even while I was still in India, my mind had already started to shift away from Bollywood, and I was starting to think more about a fitness career. I was happy. My spirits felt lifted. Just by chance – or was it chance? – I took a one-week Art of Living Course right before leaving India. And that was the next shift that took place in my mind and that pulled me deep into my soul and my spiritual path … and I have never come out of it.

After being in India for two years, I had already started preparing my mind to leave India and return to Canada in 2005. I was scared, nervous and anxious. I didn't know what I was going to do once I got to Canada. The unknown had me. However, I had my personal trainer certificate, so I went to a YMCA, told them I'd just come back from India and that I was a personal trainer, and was there any work for me there? They said, "India! Do you know yoga?" I didn't really, but my answer was a confident "YES! I know yoga!" They said, "Great! Would you like to start teaching group yoga?" My eyes must have lit up and my heart started beating fast as I anxiously said, "YES, I can teach group yoga!" They said "Great! How about starting next week?"

So I locked myself in a room for three days and studied yoga like I was cramming for college exams. Then the day arrived. I was about to teach my first class ever on something I really knew nothing about aside from the time I'd invested cramming in my room for three days. There I was with a group of twelve people in front of me, all waiting for their yoga teacher to do something. So I put on "Jai Ma" by Wah!, really just to calm myself. And I started to conduct the class with my cheat notes next to me, which I could barely see because the room had a candlelit ambiance to it. So basically I just winged it. Finally, the class ended, and I thought, "Okay, I'm fired." But then the lead instructor who hired me said, "Okay, great. We'll see you next class." Whew, I did it! Sometimes I think my life is just pure luck. But now I understand that there is no luck. Good thing the lead instructor liked me. I made it through the year teaching my yoga classes, and at the same time, I was doing personal training upstairs. Life was going smoothly, and the yogi inside me was growing day by day.

I was thirty-three at the time, and one day all of a sudden I had an abundance of energy and this idea to paint the entire basement suite I was living in. My parents were living upstairs, and I had chosen to make a little home for myself downstairs. It was a big area divided into sections, including a living area, a kitchen, a bedroom and a bathroom. But if you've ever lived in a basement suite, then you know it can be quite dim. There is not a lot of light coming in, and usually the windows are very small. I was tired of the dimness. I needed light! So I decided to get yellow paint, a soft yellow, to brighten up my living space.

I painted the entire space within three hours – a kitchen, a living room, a bedroom and a bathroom. I remember that day. I had so much energy. It was non-stop painting until I saw it was finished. There was paint all over me and my clothes, but I didn't care. I just stood back and admired it all. My place had come to life! We were speaking the same language now, me and my place. I'm a sunshine girl – I need my light. Colours have such an effect on our moods. I suppose that's why I painted like there was no tomorrow. Looking back, I don't know how I lived in the basement. But I managed, and that paint job helped a lot. "Fake" light splashed here and there over the dull walls put some life into both the place and me, which made it possible for me to keep living there a bit longer.

All was well at the YMCA until one day, while I was working as a personal trainer, a young handsome blond made eye contact with me. I'd seen him at the gym before. He called me over and said hello, so I said hi. He said, "You know, I've seen you walking around here, and you have a really pure vibe about you – you're angelic." I was speechless. I smiled big and said, "Oh yeah, thanks." He made a bit of small talk with me, and we said good-bye. From then on, I saw him at the gym again and again, and we spent all our time chatting with each other while he worked out. At the same time, I was supposed to be doing my job minding the floor and assisting people. One day he told me, "You know, I feel real good speaking with you. I feel lighter in your presence. Do you mind if we continue to speak like this whenever you're here? It helps me get through."

His statement threw me off a bit because when he said it, there was an uncomfortable wave feeling in the air. I couldn't quite figure it out – it was just an uneasy feeling. Then he grabbed my wrist abruptly and said, "Do you feel that?" My entire body felt a shock go through it like I'd had the rug pulled out from under me. I pulled back without being too obvious and still managing to keep my cool. He said, "Look at my face. Do you see my face? Do you see how one side looks evil? Look at the one side." Then he pointed to the right side of his face, and it started contorting and looking evil. Again I felt a feeling of uneasiness come over me, but I stayed calm and said, "Yeah, I think I see it." He said, "I have an evil spirit in me. Please – I need to get it out. I don't sleep at night. I've been like this for a few years. I used to be very good-looking and now – look at me." He told me his ex-girlfriend had done this to him, that she had left him with this evil spirit inside him. I calmly said, "I don't know how I can help." He said, "Just be yourself. You're a good energy. I see it all around you. You have a glow around you. Just be around me. Keep talking to me, and hopefully it will go away." I thought to myself: "If I am pure, then nothing can get me." So I said, "Okay. I'll keep talking to you." He then took it to the next level and said, "Could we meet outside the gym and go for coffee? That would be better." I said, "No, I don't want to do that, but I will come and talk to you when I'm here." So that was it.

I continued talking to him every day at the gym. He had no idea because I didn't tell him, but after he grabbed my wrist and made physical contact with me, I didn't sleep at night. I had evil spirits trying to get me. They were in my hair, on the walls, in my sheets, in my skin, pulling at me every day for a few nights. I was gone – I was not myself. I used all my yoga energy and fought it off. Finally, they went away.

Even after that, I kept talking to him at the gym, and I noticed his face getting better day by day. He was shining again. He noticed it, too. He said, "Do you see? It's better now. It's because you helped me." I smiled and said, "I'm glad I was of help." He said, "Look around you. There are many evil spirits walking the floors here." He would point at them and say, "See? Look at her. Look at him." I guess he wasn't wrong. Where there is good, there is also evil. After he got better, he didn't come back to the gym for a while. Then, one day, I saw him again. You could say he was a new birth – a charming, handsome, vibrant young guy. He came to show me. After that, he left the city. He moved away to start a new life. I wished him well, and I never saw him again.

Two years have passed. I've become a regular yoga teacher at the YMCA, and I'm enjoying every minute of it and falling more in love with the practice every day.

INDIA – FOR REAL!

Now it was only right to go back to India, this time not as an actress but as a pseudo-yogi to become the real deal. So back I went to India in 2007 to spend some time at the Yoga Institute in Mumbai, and I came back with new knowledge and a new confidence. Once back in Canada, I decided to venture out to the big gyms to do more group yoga. I did that for a few years and then went back to India in 2009 to get enlightened again. This time I was looking for meditation training. I wanted to deepen my mental power. I wanted to go for Raja Yoga. "Raja" means "king", so it's the king of yogic practices. I was eager for that. I had a keen hunger to learn the King of yogas.

I have had many gurus come into my life to help me find my spiritual self, but this particular guru who lives in Rishikesh is the one who helped me awaken my chakras. It was a hard search, but I found him. No, I did not trek through the foothills of the Himalayas or camp out in ashrams to find him. We live in a technological time, so like I said earlier, I made the connection through the internet. I started to do online searches and correspond with schools and teachers in India. Who could help me? Where in India would I go? These were the thoughts that went through my mind. I wrote emails to many teachers: "I am already a practicing yoga teacher, and I want to deepen my meditation practice by learning Raja Yoga." I finally got one response that resonated with me. The email came back, "Why do you want to learn Raja Yoga?" My answer was: "I want to go to the heights of the yogic lifestyle and practice. That's why Raja Yoga. I want the real thing, the whole thing – all of it." After a month of ongoing correspondence between me and this teacher, who is now my dear friend, my soon-to-be new teacher recommended Kundalini Tantra Yoga. So off I flew to Rishikesh, India, anxious to start my practice.

That is where it all happened. As my kundalini opened, I became enlightened. The channels of all my chakras opened. By the time I got back to Canada, I had been born anew.

My Chakra-Opening Experience

Having gone through so many other sites, I knew this teacher was the one. I knew because he asked me some personal questions about my life. I understood that these questions needed to be answered honestly and seriously. Only then could he help free me in the way I truly wished to be freed – from the emotions and senses that were governing me. What he said rang true to my ears: "Your second chakra, the sacral, or sexual, chakra needs to be worked on." I was so glad I was totally honest with him and didn't hide anything about my personal details, because he nailed it. My sexual chakra was basically in a state equivalent to an F. "Come to India, and we will work on clearing your sacral chakra." I didn't take long to say, "YES, I am coming. I will be there soon." I booked a ticket and off I went to India to free myself.

Our tantric meditative practice involved being intimate with each other. I trusted my master. I had to. I had no choice. I did not fly across the globe to fuck around. My goal was to be free, and he was supposed to help free me, so I trusted him. Extreme freedom requires extreme efforts.

We practised day after day of intimate tantric meditation. It was a lot of work. Yes, work – intimate tantric meditation is not pleasure-oriented. It is the opposite. Its purpose is to release yourself from the attachment to pleasure and go beyond it, to dive deep into a meditative trance and become one with the meditative act of intimacy. The intimacy is there to challenge you, to trick you into understanding the spiritual experience beyond just the physical, intimate level. And that's when you become free. You don't belong to the sense pleasures anymore. You have moved beyond them to your spiritual being.

Almost from the get-go of our practice, I was already free of sense pleasures. My intention was pure from the minute I got on that plane to the second I landed on Indian soil, so perhaps the Holy Lights were already with me from the beginning. I was free, but I still had to triumph over the goal that led me all the way to India. Each day I lost more and more of my attachment to the physical. Emotions and sense pleasures did not govern me anymore. All these years, I had been ruled by my emotions, and my sensuality had got the best of me. But no more. Now I was the master. I dictated the wiring within me.

So that's how it happened. I freed my quantum energies through my sacral or sexual chakra. In traditional terms, it's called raising your kundalini.

TORONTO TRANSFORMED

I still had one negative energy in my life that I needed to face. It was an energy that went against the grain of what I had just become and learned. It was a foolish love affair I had got myself into with a self-destructing soul. I had been hanging around this lost soul for two years, until 2009. I could not bring myself to forsake this being. Because of who I had become and the level I had risen to in my yogic practice, I felt it was my duty to care for and guide this lost soul. But in giving all this care, I lost all that I had captured in India. It was still there, deep down inside me. I was holding onto it for dear life, and I knew I would never lose it, but it disappeared so deep within me that I ended up in a state of temporary insanity. Now I was at war with my own being. It was a tug-of-war between purity and evil, and I felt that the evil took over the best of me. I had to get my chin back up. I had to get a grip on things, especially my mind. Never again did I let evil get me. Through a yogic lifestyle, I was able to filter the bad out of my life and see the bright lights ahead.

My mother has a shrine where she sits to do her prayers. And in the shrine she has taped pictures of all the different deities all over the walls. It looks like a really messy collage. Anyhow, there is a beautiful picture of Jesus, too, and one day, for whatever reason, I decided to click a picture of it with my BlackBerry. So I went ahead and clicked, and I was all excited to look at it in the BB photos – except there was no picture to be seen ... I was surprised for a second but then quickly understood that I had got a message from Jesus along the lines of: "You cannot click photos of me and show me off or display me. I am omnipresent, so you don't have to click me. Just know my power! I am omnipresent and omnipotent." After that, I understood and asked for forgiveness in my mind.

At certain points today, I felt the presence of a soul or atom very close to my face. I had the sensation that it was breathing on me just centimeters away. I felt a cooling sensation from it. It was very nice.

My heart rate also sped up at times. I could separate my physical self and my mental self from each other. There was no attachment to either.

I saw a pink light around myself while my eyes were shut. It was a radiant bright pink light. I just saw a few quick flashes of it.

I zoned out everything around me. No voices, dialogue, images, emotions – nothing … just being. No mind. I came into a dialogue for a second and quickly snapped out of it and back into nothingness.

I dreamt I expelled a huge, disgusting chunk of phlegm from my lungs. It was almost unbearable. Today, on 26 March, I actually did expel a massive, ugly piece of phlegm from my lungs. It was unimaginable to me that an alien substance like that could come out of me. I understand it, though. It's my kundalini rising – the depths of meditation clearing out the last of the toxins from my body … kundalini, in full motion, cleaning me out.

Let's back up a bit. One important point is that I just finished nine days of Navratri fasting, part of the Navratri festival honoring Shakti. There was no meat eating, which is another means of cleansing that works hand in hand with the kundalini meditation process. Shakti gave me her blessings, meaning that the fast I was respectfully observing by giving something up for nine days was accepted by the universe. I was in sync with the positive side of the law of attraction. Shakti is a powerful female energy. It is also a creative energy, the feminine aspect of yin and yang, night and day, male and female.

LONDON

I still wasn't able to concentrate on my awakened third-eye chakra that had opened in India. It was still suppressed. I decided to just let it be and let time bring it back to me. Next thing I knew I was on a plane moving to London, England, in October 2010, to get married because of an arranged setup that had happened a few months back in August of the same year. It was the most impulsive, spontaneous decision I'd ever made. I saw the guy for a few days, we liked each other, and that was it. We said, "Okay, let's tell the family were doing it. We're getting married." We were so above ourselves, we went to Miami's famous South Beach to get hitched. Called all our family there and had a pastor read us our vows. There we were, getting married under the light of the sky on a sandy beach in Miami, Florida, within arm's length of the beautiful ocean in November 2010.

Well, that didn't last too long. We were separated by June 2011. A whole seven months of marriage, Hollywood-style. And the split was even grander. Sitting at a Café de Paris in Monte Carlo, we watched the Ferraris, Lamborghinis and Aston-Martins showcase their masses of metal as we sipped our juice and went over the final details of our split and the valid reasons we had for it.

I have to admit – it was bittersweet. It was a mindf#% at times prior to the final sit-down at the Café de Paris in Monaco. This was supposed to be our honeymoon trip, because we never had one in Miami. Miami was all about drinks and other people. From Miami, we came back to the UK and planned a real honeymoon with just the two of us – no crowds of people. I had no idea what was coming. Things were really rocky before we left, but we decided to go, anyway, since the trip was already booked. It was for three nights and four days in Nice, Cannes and Monaco.

Being on a trip with my so-called husband but not being able to show any signs of affection, not having any conversations, sleeping in the same bed but finding an invisible barrier between us – sharing a hotel room under these strict conditions was like a slow kill, but later, to my surprise (or was it a surprise?), I found that the split-up was actually a blessing. Sometimes we subconsciously sabotage our own situations or relationships because we know we're not really meant to be in them. To close a chapter with solidity is a breath of fresh air. It was okay to be in beautiful Monaco and enjoy the grand scale of it and, on the other hand, to find solace and peace of mind in the acknowledgement that all things must come to an end.

I realized that this whole domestic ordeal was irrelevant on one level, while on another level, it was a significant part of the spiritual calling that had been awaiting me. This process had to happen to validate my sense of who and what I was. A strong pull arose within me almost immediately, from day one of this consummation. But I had to learn the hard way, and I got the confirmation that this lifestyle was not for me. My purpose and calling were of the higher self, the spiritual nature. I needed to be with my spiritual gods, who were waiting for me with open arms. My third eye was open again, now that I was free from domestic entanglements. When we got back to London, I packed up my stuff and left for India.

Fire

She's fire …
it's hard to put her out.
She brings on heat …
I'm trying to keep up …

I feel choked.
I want her flame to die,
but she never dims.

I'm getting frustrated …
put her flame out …

but wait – don't I need it … ?

If I tried to prevent myself from eating meat, then I would not be myself. I would be an impersonator. I don't rely on it, but when I desire it, I have it. So far, this has in no way hindered my spirituality and my yoga path. My calling is to remain as I am and teach what I know. Many spiritual leaders in history have been known to be carnivores. It never made them bad people for doing so. I am on exactly my right path. I am not living a clichéd life.

I know who and what I am, and that is exactly what yoga practice wants you to achieve – to find your higher self through being yourself. Don't get too caught up in what is expected of you or what others wish to see. Be true to who you are – that is pure in itself.

Jesus ate meat. That didn't make him a non-spiritual leader. Many Buddhists eat meat. The way I see it, you should eat what is put in front of you. If you were in a desert, and the only things in sight were ants, spiders, and other insects, and if you needed to eat them to survive, would you? I would. But I am not scared of death – it doesn't bother me. So if I just couldn't bring myself to eat the insects, then I would be prepared to die.

When things went bad in the UK, I ended up in hospital. The build-up to it was slow. The week before that, I remember walking around the streets of London feeling ever so tired. I could not walk fast, the way I normally do. I could not make it up the subway stairs. I had to let others pass me by. It was embarrassing and sad. I did not understand what was going on with my body. It was very hard to breathe, too. Every breath took so much out of me that I barely made it back home to Ealing. I had to stop every three minutes to catch my breath, and if I couldn't find a bench to sit down on, I crouched down on the ground. Passersby looked at me strangely. They knew something was obviously not right, but they were helpless to do anything for me. I don't blame them. I didn't know what to do for myself.

This went on for a good week or so. I had gone to my cousin's place for a sleepover, and he saw me struggling, trying to get up his flight of ten stairs. He said, "What's wrong with you? Can't you get up this small set of steps?" I said, "No, I'm finding it very hard," and once again I sank down to rest. At least, it was not a public sidewalk this time. My aunt and he pulled out an inhaler test, and I failed to breathe well. The average breath is supposed to be something like 400 or above, and mine was 75. They decided then and there that I needed to go to hospital. I didn't fight it. I just said "Okay." My cousin is a funny guy, a great joker, so when he and I were in the car, he kept saying, "Just fake it, and fake it even more when we get there! Maybe we can bypass the emergency line." Well, I was trying to be a good sport and laugh a little with him, but I explained to him, "I'm not faking it – this is real. I really can't breathe."

When we got to the hospital, there must have been at least twenty people standing ahead of me in the emergency line, some in wheelchairs, some with bleeding arms. The procedure is that you go to the reception desk first, and the nurse asks you, "What's the emergency?" Well, I certainly didn't look like there was anything wrong with me. There was a calmness in my face, so the nurse kind of looked at me like, "I don't think you belong here." I opened my mouth and said three words, "I can't breathe." She stared at me for a few seconds, realized that there was some paleness in my face, hooked up this unit to my finger to test the oxygen levels in my blood, and then went into panic mode – more than I was. Then she gave me the same breath test that I'd done at my cousin's place, and it still read 75.

So there we were. Right away I bypassed the twenty people with their bleeding arms and wheelchairs, and the next thing I knew I was lying on a hospital bed with an oxygen tank hooked up to my mouth. The nurses kept saying, "Breathe! Keep breathing deeply." And that I did very well. I don't think my yoga skills had ever been tested so much as they were at that very moment. I knew how to relax. I knew how to breathe. I did not panic.

This went on for days. I was in the hospital for almost two weeks. By the time the respiratory doctor came around to see me, it had already been three days. One of the first things he said was, "How did you manage to survive breathing like this for such a long period of time? Your records show that you said you haven't been breathing well for over ten days or so." I said, "Well, I'm a yogini. I'm a practitioner of yoga disciplines, including meditative breathing practices." He said, "If it weren't for your practice, who knows ..."

Basically, I had a second chance at life, thanks to my practice. I called the yoga that I taught at the time "Breath Yoga", and this event was a testament to the validity of the yoga system. It supported me for all those days, even though I was struggling. It stuck by me. I may have been walking at turtle speed, but at least I wasn't dead. Ending up in hospital was a blessing. It helped me get my lungs back in shape, which is why they decided to keep me there so long – to make sure that my lungs were in excellent condition so that I could have my life back.

It was an insightful experience, my stay in hospital. I never treated the hospital experience like a bad one. I fully embraced the hospital life. It was what it was, so I figured I might as well have a good attitude about it. The doctors were there to help me, and because I believed this, the hospital was not such a bad place to be. I had very sick, even dying respiratory patients all around me. All of them were stuck in their beds 24/7 with oxygen tanks. That meant that I had my own personal shower, as every other patient in my ward was bedridden. I would get up with energy, happy to take my towel and toothbrush to the shower, where I would take my time and embrace the experience of hospital life for the days I was there. I brought my good energy into the place. I figured the people there could use it, so I made friends with the patients around me. I did my yoga asanas every day on the bed, and I tried to spread my energy, my love and my compassion to all around me. I smiled from my bed, and they smiled back. When my release date came, I was happy to go home – well, actually, there was no home. Instead, I went to India. I had booked my ticket just a few days before being admitted to the hospital, and once I was on my way, I never looked back. Life was what it was, and now I could see the present and the future as I looked forward to India.

INDIA AGAIN GETTING BACK THE MAGIC

I left for India in July 2011. I stayed there for three months and started teaching yoga classes in Delhi. I got tired of Delhi city life, though – the traffic, the pollution, the honking cars that sounded like really old 1940s horns piercing your eardrums. From there, I made my way to serene Rishikesh. Finally, the magic started again in Rishikesh. I got my third-eye kundalini back. I practised with the same teacher I had had before, who had also become a dear friend by this time. We practised kundalini and chakras, and finally I got it back. My peer recognized that I had it. He said, "You are not the same person who came to me a couple of years back. You are in true form now." I was happy that he saw it. What he didn't know was that my kundalini had been so hidden. I had dug for it and prayed for it, but it had only emerged just now, on this trip, so I was ecstatic after having it hidden for so long. My thoughts had been: "I'm seeing my peer after such a long time, and I don't know if my enlightened glow is still there", but he never knew I had misplaced it.

What great timing for it to come back to me now! I was finally in my element again, after all the turbulence of the last two years. Perhaps that was what made it come back to me. I was so joyful over that great moment that I felt I had to go to the mountains near the Ganga (Ganges). I packed up, left my teacher's place and stayed at an ashram in the hillside area of Rishikesh. I was exactly where I wanted to be, surrounded by trees, the Ganga and the mountain terrain. I met some nice students at the ashram – nobody fascinating, but nice students.

I was a student, too. Sometimes I just like to remain a humble student and learn from fellow yogis. I was interested in the main guru of the ashram, the laughing yogi. I found him to be fun and light. He was always laughing and smiling. I loved his energy and found myself falling for him, or perhaps it was his joy that was rubbing off on me. I think I have a weak spot for all the fellow yogis I encounter. Their auras are captivating. I met the laughing yogi while I was with another yogi peer. We sat in the entrance lobby and exchanged some nice words with each other. I didn't reveal much to him about the fact that I also taught yoga disciplines, but we did share a common link: he travels to Canada as well. He was kind and invited my peer and me to dinner at the ashram. He joined us as we ate. He didn't eat a morsel of food but gave us his ever so loving and cheerful company. The next day, I brought my belongings and stayed there for a couple of nights. I saw the yogi again on my own this time. We spent some time talking, and then I told him that I was a Kundalini Tantra Yoga teacher. He took note of me from head to toe, making his observations of me, I guess. I didn't mind. After all, we're all human.

98

After that, he left on a trip and would be back to teach in a few days. I stayed at the ashram, waiting for his arrival so I could take his class. During the three days I was there, I met again with my yogi peer, who introduced me to a number of fellow yogis, including one who was just around the corner from the ashram where I was staying. We went in and sat down, and when he greeted us, I was swept away by him, too. He was simple, with beautiful long hair, but he had this very noticeable diamond ring on his finger. I pointed it out to him and said, "Why do you wear that?" He was smart. He answered the question with a question and said, "Why do you think I wear it?" I found that to be so mind-stimulating. And totally diplomatic – perhaps something I would have said, too. Maybe that's why he became a favorite of mine so soon. I liked his overall way of speaking. He seemed like a wise yogi. I'll call him "the diamond yogi". He was a to-the-point kind of yogi who didn't waste time and didn't do what he didn't wish to do. My peer kept probing him about teaching more classes, but he handled it well. I went the next day on my own and brought one of the students from the ashram who was interested in meeting a good yogi. I told him, "I know one. Let me take you to him. I don't know if he'll let us in because he doesn't know you, but let's see." He didn't let us in. I sensed that "diamond yogi" was happy to see me but not the student I'd brought along. He gave us some time, answered the student's questions, and off we went.

When I came home, I emailed him: "I hope I didn't offend you by bringing my student along." He emailed me back, saying he hoped he hadn't been rude to him. I was thrilled that he responded – we we're making the connection. I replied, "No, you were not rude at all. You said what you felt. You were diplomatic, and that's okay." I also felt quite honored that he was taking my advice and asking for my approval on things. It made me realize that I also had the yogi being within me.

In the meantime, the happy-go-lucky, cheerful yogi had come back from his trip, so I was excited. I did his class with great pleasure. I think I must have been radiating kundalini energy in my exuberance, because he looked my way a lot. At one point, he came over to correct my pose. He was so close to me that I felt each breath of his, and he too felt my energy intertwining and blending with his own. It was magnetic. I will never forget it. I even wrote him an email about it. He never wrote me back, but that's okay. He's probably being a disciplined yogi by keeping his distance.

Feeling fulfilled by the whole experience, I soon needed to venture out again. My heart desired Osho. I wanted to do something related to his practices – to find an Osho ashram, if I could be so lucky. The next thing I knew, I was leaving the ashram for a walk when an older man came up to me out of the blue and handed me a pamphlet about Osho meditation. The pamphlet showed all the Osho practices and how to do them, like a teach-yourself guide. I was happy to receive it from him, but at the same time I felt dejected because I didn't want to do them myself. I wanted to be properly guided at an Osho ashram. It was something I had never experienced before, and I felt I would be happy being an honest-to-goodness student.

As I was walking, just by chance – or was it by chance? – I looked up and saw a sign for an Osho Dham (ashram). I lit up. I felt elated again. Right away I started following the arrows to find it, but with no luck. I was too far away, which made it hard to locate, so I asked the people I met while I was walking. People would give me wrong directions, but I just kept going. Finally, a man on a motorbike said, "Hey, where are you going? There's nothing this way." I said, "I'm trying to find the Osho Dham. I saw signs for it." He was kind enough to say, "Hop on. I'll take you there." He took me to a pathway close to the Ganga, so I walked down to the river – and there it was. After looking around a while, I finally found someone. He was the keeper of the ashram and a practising sannyasi. His name was Dilip, a nice-looking, clean-shaven young guy with glowing dark, smooth skin. I enquired about staying, then came back the next day, stayed a couple of nights and got to do all the practices. It was so liberating.

After that, I went back to the central Rishikesh area, where I decided to see the long-haired yogi with the diamond ring one last time to say my good-byes before heading back to Delhi. He welcomed me and showed me his new ashram that he was setting up. He was happy to see that I admired his studio. We said good-bye, and he said, "Let's see if we ever meet again." I said, "I'm sure we will someday."

Life has been good to me. I've managed to become self-taught in a few things. I guess it had to be that way, considering I had no guidance growing up. I'm not educated in terms of degrees but in terms of life itself.

I love to cook Indian and Western food. I remember making my first dal while I was living in a tenth-floor flat in Versova, in Mumbai. I was just winging it and wanted to see how the dal turned out. It turned out beautifully. I was ecstatic. Of course, some credit should go to Mother for the times I watched over her shoulder to see how she did it. I guess I intuitively knew I would be living a solitary life in the coming days and years – for the most part, anyhow – so I figured I'd better learn to cook.

I learned how to swim in the pools of Mumbai. Mumbai has what they call private membership clubs. I would go there and try my luck at swimming, and I finally grasped it. It was a joyful moment. I have always been afraid of swallowing too much water, but I finally got the hang of breathing in and out the right way. We had to learn how to swim in school. I made it to the red level, which is considered okay, but I just couldn't get past red. My arms would be all over the place, and my breathing had no system. I was like a panting pup in the water. So it was quite a moment for me when I finally grasped the technique in the pools of the Lokhandwala Complex in Mumbai.

I also thought that because I was studying yoga, I obviously had to learn the famous yoga headstand. So it was practise, practise, practise until I finally got it. I'm still not perfect at it. I try to stay up there for a while, but I tend to fall down quickly. But I still keep plugging away.

Then there was my business training. Since I never went to business school – or any school, really – I had to learn about managing a small business in my home yoga studio. It's been trial and error and still is, but I learn a little more each time. Sometimes it feels like I'm not getting anywhere, but perhaps that's the fire that keeps moving me ahead.

A selfish being

A selfish being,
he loves to destroy you
with smooth, alluring words
that captivate.

You buy in ... and next,
he's sunk into your brain.

He toys with you.
Oh, isn't it fun!
Dangle,
entangle them.
Oh, isn't it fun ...

Truth unveils

He told me his secrets.
I told him mine.
But we just couldn't bind.

He wanted to claim
she's mine mine mine
Turns out, she's only the world's ...
And everything's fine.

Empty walls, a mental asylum –
That's what they were.
Cloak and dagger,
they pointed at her
to be the nagger.

Slick, sly –
he's not so fly ...
Riches to rage.

He promised her
golden forests and silver seas
What a tease ...

He silently offered the crazy cage
She naturally raged

For in the end, she walks alone ...
It is her fate.
So why hate?

While I was in India for my personal meditation retreat, I made some friends who also became what Indians call "good friends", meaning lovers. One of the relationships was a tantric experience that I guess I was testing in my own way, but the person I was with didn't know that. There's always a method to my madness. I simply wanted to see if I could handle this kind of thing mentally. Could I love many souls at one time? Could I love them all evenly and full-heartedly? Could I detach from the last person I shared my light with? Could I express a different love with each soul?

I was completely satisfied with the answers to all my questions. There was no wrongdoing in my mind. It was all perfectly perfect. When you become free of your attachments, there's plenty of love to go around, and it can take many forms and have many dynamics. It's a beautiful gift to have. Each relationship has its time for being fully in the moment, and when that moment is over, you move on. If you can realize that the time for the relationship is over, and you can detach yourself from it, that relationship becomes a lifelong friendship, and it ends up having more value than the ones that you try to cling to or force into a specific mode.

The night before my flight to London, I returned to Delhi, where I also stayed at the Osho ashram. And that is where I met Mr. Sweden, a handsome, young, blue-eyed Swedish guy. We met at the Osho ashram in Delhi on 3 October 2011. We met for just a few moments at first. It started with only a few glances exchanged in the Osho bookshop. He was on the other side of the glass playing childlike games with me, like "peek-a-boo I-see-you". I thought he was a one-of-a-kind, interesting character that I would like to know better. We exchanged just a few words over lunch, and the next moment we were out gallivanting across Delhi together.

We spent the whole day in each other's light and found ourselves unable to part from each other as the Delhi night glared upon us. We got a nice little hotel room, which we had trouble finding because in India they don't allow a man and woman to crash in the same room together unless they're married. So we were wandering around the tourist district of Delhi trying to figure out what to do, and it wasn't looking very hopeful. And then – can you believe it? – someone started shouting my name: "Reyna! Reyna!" I looked to see who was calling me, and it happened to be the guy who worked at the grocery store in Janak Puri. He was dressed in business attire, so I didn't recognize him, because he wasn't wearing his usual grungy grocery store clothing. He said to me, "What are you doing here in Pahar Ganj?" Pahar Ganj is the area with lots of tourist hotels and shops, and you find more foreigners there than locals. He was shocked to see me there because it was miles away from where I was staying in Janak Puri. I pointed to my lovely Swedish friend and said, "I'm here with my friend, and we're trying to get a hotel room." He said, "Oh, great! You can stay here at my hotel." He pointed behind him. Mr. Sweden and I looked at each other in shock: "OMG, can you believe how this happened …!" It was unreal. The grocery store guy turned out to be more than a grungy fruit stocker, after all. It was his dad's hotel, which he managed when he wasn't doing shifts at the grocery store. So there we were, unmarried, an Indian girl and a Swedish guy getting a room together in Delhi … it's unheard of! All thanks to "coincidentally" running into someone I knew. Life's got to make you laugh!

India was great for the three months I spent there but I was getting really tired of all the hustling. I kept thinking, "I can't do this again ... I can't keep hopping into bumpy rickshaw rides going from one place to the next." Sure, I had respected work in Delhi. I was the so-called director of yoga activities for over eight of their chain fitness clubs – part of The Gym. But you would never know it. My rides back and forth between locations were far from travelling in style. I had to do a lot of bumpy, dusty commuting in auto-rickshaws from one club to the next. It brought me back to my Mumbai days. A lot of well-to-do people do commute by auto-rickshaw. Sometimes it's just easier than taking your car. You can eliminate heavy traffic and parking issues, especially in a densely populated country like India. But I was tired of subpar commuting all the time!

It was this one particular incident that really did it. I was sitting in a rickshaw that was stopped at a red light with a hundred other cars all around me. Well, in India, people stare. It's allowed! It's almost strange if you don't stare at other cars when you're stopped at a red light. Because I was in a rickshaw, which is all open – no hiding in that thing – I felt a lot of eyes on me. So I casually turned my head from side to side, looking here and there, and I noticed a car to my right. A beautiful, expensive car – some European make. And the guy inside the car was a well-to-do guy. Mostly people in India in these high-end cars have it all. In fact, they don't drive the cars themselves. They have drivers. That's probably why they're busy people watching.

At that moment, everything hit me – and it hit hard. I was so embarrassed to be traveling by rickshaw. For the first time in my life, I pitied myself, and I am not one for self-pity. I felt embarrassed that I had evolved so much in my life's path and was still traveling by bloody rickshaw. And I knew that guy was looking at me like he was thinking "She doesn't look like the type to be in a rickshaw." All of a sudden, I felt the blood rush into my face when the light turned green. My bumpy rickshaw ride started put-putting in the heavy Delhi traffic. I tried to look composed and suave, like the guy in his luxury car next to me. But I couldn't. I was in a rickshaw! Once my put-putmobile was away from all the traffic, I just let go. My eyes filled with tears, and I had my private beef with the gods. "What are you doing to me? I can't keep doing this. Don't you think I've had enough?"

Soon after that I got a call from my cousin Vinny in New York. (Just kidding.) I got a call from my cousin in NYC, and he said, "What are you doing in India? Come back! Come here to New York if you don't want to go to Toronto, and we'll figure things out for you here in NYC." It was music to my ears to hear that. I didn't have a game plan for New York, but I felt the love just knowing I had people in my life who cared about me. And New York sounded like heaven after what I just experienced. He kept saying, "Just come! We'll make it work. How can you live there? It must be so tough over there. Just come to New York."

And that was it. I soon made arrangements to pack up India, and I headed to

NYC. There I was again, going across the globe – first from West to East, then back again, from East to West. I was basically coming full circle, back to North America again.

Sometimes the people who are closest to you are terrified of your success. Sometimes, too, the strangers we meet or work with will tell us, "Is that all you've got?" Don't let it confuse you. They're telling you this because you have value, and they're boosting you up.

You are light.
They want you to shine ...
encouraging you to give all you've got!

And if for some reason
you think they want to discourage you ...

Be quiet.
Observe.
Let them speak
and say what they have to say.

They want to see you defeated.
But you know your own light.
And so do they.

Sometimes we just need to take a moment to read our fellow beings. And if you think positively you can see the beautiful message in all things.

God, the universe, the mighty atoms or electrons, or whatever you want to call it, gives me everything I want. I have never really prayed at any mandir, temple or other religious place. I ask from my heart, and I am given. There were even some things that I was curious about but didn't really want, and I was given those, too. So now I am careful about what I ask for.

Learn to slow down! Especially New Yorkers! Running all the time, making money, making babies, etc. ... Even I am still learning to slow down. When I'm asked to teach an hour-and-a-half class, I have to consciously slow down. You will still accomplish the things you want to do if you slow down. You'll be more concentrated, and your ideas will be better thought out.

The mind of an Indian Woman

I am proud to be Canadian-Indian, but there are some rituals in Indian culture that I don't agree with. I guess those things are not in line with a yogic lifestyle, which is something beautiful that also originated in India.

The Indian woman never lives for herself – she lives for her husband. It is absolutely wrong. She is so desperate to know his each and every move. She is way too attached and obviously not practising the way of pratyahara, or the detachment of the senses and emotions. She has forgotten about herself and her identity, so she becomes ill. All kinds of diseases and mental illnesses arise within the Indian woman. She doesn't realize that her husband is living his own life. He is not interested in her – ever – so she finds herself dying of love for him. That doesn't turn him on! On top of it all, to make things even more ridiculous, there is a fast that happens once a year called Karva Chauth, which degrades the woman even more. She starves herself all day for the sake of her husband's health and longevity. Again, the poor woman doesn't stand a chance. Her Indian culture degrades her by never allowing her to be on a par with her male counterpart.

I'm an Indian woman, too. I love my Indian sisters. I want to give them shakti and make them strong – to empower them to make a difference and not be so timid and shy but to come out, come out, wherever you are ... Face the world – don't hide! Shine, my sisters!

That Saturday night, I was going on a date, and I was waiting to meet him at the bar across from Penn Station. There was a couple sitting beside me, and all of a sudden the tiny Asian woman started speaking to me. "Hey, where are you from?" I was surprised, because in New York, everyone keeps to themselves. You're lucky if you get a smile out of a New Yorker. I told her I'd just moved from London and had kind of been all over the world – India, London and now here. She seemed pleasantly surprised, and she became chummy with me from that point on. Next thing I knew, she was making me a plate of sausages and fries and slid it over to me. "Here you go. Eat these – they're really good." Now that NEVER happens in the Big Apple, and once again, my life was full of good stuff.

I was on the LIRR from Penn station going back to Long Island. A cute mid-thirties Asian girl sat down beside me and wouldn't stop talking. I was looking for some quiet time, a little tranquility. It was late, and I just wanted to keep to my meditative self. But it was okay – she was nice, so I opened my heart to her. She was comparing the Chinese political system to the U.S one. She wasn't impressed with American political policies and ways of operating. I didn't blame her. Then she pulled out her iPad and showed me pics of her baby, so I had to just go with it. She wanted to share – so be it. Finally, she got around to asking me what I did. I told her I was a yoga teacher. She took a huge gasp of air out of excitement. I wasn't feeling too great about the day's events, so I didn't react much to her excitement. I asked her about her profession and found out that she was a postdoctoral fellow, a bioengineer. Now *that* was impressive to me. I guess we were each impressed by what the other did. She did manage to lift my spirits a bit. She complimented me by saying that I had a totally artsy look, and that was music to my ears. I would never want to be told that I looked conservative, which I am not. How you dress and your overall style can represent whatever message you send out – it's fascinating stuff.

It was cool that she recognized some creative quality in me. Something made me give her my business card, maybe because she complimented me. That made her really happy. It was interesting to watch her hang onto it, like someone had given her a piece of jewelry to hold onto and she had to be very careful with it. She made it a point to look down at the card every few seconds. It was fulfilling to watch. That's when I realized that I must have been emanating some inner light. It made my day.

HOME TO TORONTO

I'm off to Toronto now after spending two months in New York. I guess I didn't do too badly there. Prior to that, I spent three months in India and a few days in London. I couldn't seem to find much yoga work in New York, so I didn't want to float around the Big Apple too much longer. I have a feeling that I won't be staying in Toronto too long, either – maybe a couple of months again, and then we'll see where the wild wind takes me next! I'll stay if I can find the right people, the kind who understand me and want to work with me in a consistent manner. If not, once again I'll fly away like a little butterfly!

I spent my New Year's Eve exactly as I wanted to, at home by myself, with my parents around for part of the evening and the rest of it all to myself. I had my pre-New Year's Eve celebration the night before, on Friday, December 30. I had met a student, or you could also say that he was a friend of mine. We planned to spend the entire night at a hotel, where we would love each other and be companions for that one night. It was great! We said our good-byes the next morning and left each other with a deep understanding of love and friendship.

I wanted to spend New Year's Eve 2011 by myself because I felt it was the calm before the storm. The year 2012 was going to be filled with a new joy, colour, lights, cameras, speeches, loudness. All the inner preparations I'd had brewing in my head for so long were about to come to life. The omnipotent and omnipresent Light had been preparing me for it. I watched a bit of the movie *Studio 54* tonight. It was a good way for me to pump myself up for my present mindset because it's about a kid from Jersey with big dreams of New York. He goes through a lot of hardship but makes it in the end.

After that, I watched some documentary on Marilyn Monroe. I see shades of who I am in all people, as we are all light and energy. I enjoy watching films and seeing how I fit into some of the characters people play. Or I like watching autobiographies of remembered souls. Marilyn Monroe was a sensual energy who spread her exuberance to the world but who also conveyed innocence. She wouldn't hurt anyone. She only cared about and loved the people who came into her life.

I cracked open the fortune cookie I ate today, and the little paper read: "You will move to a wonderful new home within the year." Ha! It made me chuckle. Of course, I was happy to read it, but I know you can't always believe what these little scripts say. However, it's good to be optimistic. I do see a house or ashram by the seaside.

Lately, I have had consecutive dreams where Neil, my brother, has been appearing. This is unusual. Normally, he would come into my dreams when I was really down and out or totally confused about someone or something. Then he'd come into my dreams, and I'd get my answers. But lately he's been coming for a few days in a row. He knew my mind's plans. It was like he was telling me, "Keep going – you're doing good." In my dream, he said, "I love you, Charu." That was the first time ever he'd said such a thing – ever.

Also, about this writing that I'm doing … He knows what I am writing, and he is proud that I am doing it. I am sharing our childhood – letting our story out, sharing it with the world. It's not just my story but his and mine. It's very cool. I like that he's been in my dreams. It's giving me great power to make things happen. I will do what needs to be done.

My life is never boring. I choose it to be what I want it to be. Life is about having a beautiful time together to create lasting memories. What's all the hype about New Year's, anyhow? People get all done up, go to big parties, get completely smashed and don't remember a thing, The New Year should be brought in so that you have time to reflect on your year, have some soul time with yourself – perhaps look up at the sky and think about what you would like to see happen this year. If you hit a big party with pretentious people and lots of fake laughter and cheering, I think you'd somehow still feel empty at the end of the night. And you'd feel even worse the next morning when you woke up with a hangover.

People don't usually say what they mean. As a gesture of politeness, when someone is about to hang up the phone, they say, "Give my regards to your family", but they don't really mean it. And the person on the receiving end says, "Sure, I will", but they never do. It just goes to show you that the world is not real. It's made up of many fake gestures. So don't let yourself be so drawn into everything you hear.

There is a saying from the movie *Miami Vice:* "Leave now. Life is short. Time is luck." I love this saying. However, there is no luck. The Divine Light makes us move and shifts our lives around to get us to the right places and to make the right things happen.

I was standing in the kitchen with my mother, and she called me GOD! Ha ha, lol – and it was for real! She didn't realize she had called me that. She said it in Hindi, which is Rab. I mentioned it to her, saying, "Do you realize that you just called me GOD? She said, "No, I just called you, and that came out of my mouth." Lol! I guess I have that effect on her. And I know the Supreme Light, which some call God, is always with me.

I was sitting in my room in silence. I was in my own zen. I looked up at the mirror, where I have a photo of Radha Krishna. Radha is Krishna's lover. I noticed the photo was upside down …? It made me chuckle to myself because things like this are the norm in my life. I realized it was a message from Krishna, but I couldn't figure out what the message meant. Then I got it – I knew. I have a note on the same mirror right across from Radha Krishna's photo, and the note was important to me. It was a reminder of things that I wished for in my life. So the photo of Krishna facing upside down was telling me: "We got it. We know what you want, and we support you."

So that was clear – I got that message from the photo being turned upside down. But then I thought to myself, "There must be another message in this." So I picked up the photo, which is actually a business card, and I turned it over and saw the name of a website. I then checked out the site, which was a Hare Rama Hare Krishna temple in West Virginia, but nothing particularly stood out to me about the site. However, it showed the farm where they took care of the cows – not for meat, of course, but for milk only, I believe. So the message I got out of that was that I was on the right track with my diet. I had taken up sattvic eating at the time, which means no meat, fish, or eggs. So seeing the cows was a reminder to me that Krishna knew what I was up to and saw I had given up non-veg foods, and also that he saw the note on the mirror and acknowledged all things. The only way of letting me know that he knew was by flipping the picture upside down!

According to Einstein, our brains put out a frequency, which is picked up by other brains or consciousnesses with the same type of energy. That passes through the ether, and it bypasses space and time. Krishna is pure consciousness. Krishna does not need a physical form to see what is going on. He is consciousness, and so are you, so you can vibrate with Krishna anytime. All the mighty beings that walked our earth, like Krishna and Jesus, all have consciousness. They see, and they vibrate. And you, too, have consciousness. You, too, vibrate and can vibrate with them at their frequencies.

I heard Comedian Ricky Gervais quote John Wooden on a talk show when he said, "Ability is a poor man's wealth." Well, isn't that true! I have led such a colourful life that I have never had a dull moment. I have learned so much from my global travels and the people I've met. They say that life is not always what it seems … isn't that true, too! Not a single person's status in life can faze me, because I understand that we are all just energies and made of the same thing. The status you hold is temporary.

Actually, everything is temporary, so there's no need to get so attached to it. That means that I and a Hollywood actor or the President of the U.S. are all the same with regard to our energy and being. If you can keep this way of thinking in mind, you'll never sink in life. By the way, I will say that I do love the U.S. President. I am so proud that I live in this time and that I got to witness the first black President of America – Barack Obama. He got elected first in 2008 for a four-year term and now again in 2012 for another four years. I have been part of this historical moment, and I am so proud of it.

Taking things a little deeper, I'm proud that I walk the earth where great people have walked before me – like Mother Therese of Germany, who would pour out blood every Friday for the son of God, Jesus. He gave her this gift, and yes, she saw it as a gift from Jesus. She accepted that she had been chosen to prove his existence – that he was once here and that he did in fact shed a lot of blood on the cross. So every Friday Mother Therese poured out blood. It was something she could not control – it just happened. You could say that it was God-sent. And Paramahansa Yoganandaji saw this happen. Paramahansa Yoganandaji was a well-known yoga guru and philosopher who came to America in the early 1900s to teach Westerners about yoga. He taught the philosophy of Kriya Yoga. He met Mother Therese of Germany. He went there from America and spent a few days with her to witness this miraculous experience of blood pouring out of her body.

These are the great people who walked our earth, and we can learn from them. We are all energies, and we all work in the same way. Through my experiences with yoga and meditation, I have learned that the ability of knowing beyond, knowing the inner person, is there for all of us to explore.

As I delve deeply into my oceanic mind in various states of meditation, I come to new conclusions about life and about my own path and how I am going about it. I have realized as I go more and more into seclusion that I find it at times challenging to conduct the meditation programmes I have created. At present I have created a Kundalini Tantra meditation workshop, and I encourage yoga studios to allow me to come and teach the knowledge of this practice. In the last few weeks, I have been in an oceanic state of meditation. It has given me new perspectives on how to teach my workshops, which is exciting for me, as I am able to keep reinventing myself. Perhaps as I keep delving more and more into this ethereal mind, I will change my teachings again!

Wonderful new beliefs and pure impulses have arisen from my practice, such as all of a sudden deciding to not eat eggs, meat, and fish. It wasn't a struggle. It happened effortlessly. In the blink of an eye, I no longer ate these foods. It has been about one month since this new diet, and I am loving it. I feel closer to my beliefs about the Omnipotent. I feel the light of the Omnipotent pulling me closer to it. It is clearly saying to me, "The time has come to pull you towards me. You're coming to me to spread the light!"

I also realize I am here to be a modern yogi for the 21st century, to lead the people of today on a path of enlightenment. People today are hip, and everybody is a rock star, so having a modern yogi is absolutely necessary to get the attention of the people of today's world. It's also proof that a hip yogi can exist in the 21st century. They will exist as long as this material world is moving, and yogis will keep appearing in all eras and adapting to the times. In every era, everything is and will be omnipotent and omnipresent.

I happen to have been blessed with the opportunity to witness the turn of the 21st century. I couldn't be more blessed. We are all blessed to have been a part of that – to be alive at this time. How amazing is that! It is a historic part of being here on earth. How many people get to experience what we in this era got to experience? This is a time of great changes, and it is a true blessing to be present in such a great century, when the world is changing so fast. It's a time of technological milestones, of robots cleaning your floors for you. So what about going back to the basics? We've gone so far from them and are going even further, as the world is moving so fast with machines, computers and technology. But we need to be grounded to build our foundation, which is our spirituality – because that will take us to the top.

This present time is also the Kali Yuga, which means that it's a time of recession, unemployment, low income and global warming. It's a difficult race to be the best. You need to be above your game and above your will to be successful in the corporate world or even to just maintain your day job as a laborer, teacher or whatever you might be. This is not the era for laziness. This era, more than ever, requires guidance to lead us back to the basics and to ground ourselves, which comes from making the effort towards a spiritual connection.

17 May 2012 – I'm A Seasoned Soul!

As I was practicing meditation today, I was enlightened as to who I was and how long I have been here. I am an old, old soul. I have been here for over 200,000 years, since back when the human species first arrived as Neanderthals. I was a male Neanderthal. Perhaps that explains my interest in shakti and my present-day path to spirituality, since this soul has experienced the cycle of birth and death for centuries. I believe the Neanderthals were vegetarians as well, contrary to the common belief that they were carnivores. Perhaps being vegetarian on and off, which happens quite effortlessly, is just right for me, considering who I was. We had to eat leaves and plants and whatever we could find. I have perhaps gone back to some of my original ways. I have had many other bodies and forms, but this is the one that has come to light so far.

DHARAMSALA

Dharamsala, India, 9 June 2012

My experience this time in India was different from any other I've had. It was the first time I had ever been to Dharamsala. I had never been to the extreme northern part of India before. It is a beautiful, mountainous region. There is lovely, clean air up there, which is a blessing for the respiratory system.

I also had the company of a fellow yogi. I call this yogi "the ageless yogi". He's "the ageless yogi" because I don't know how old he is, and whenever I ask, I never get an answer. Not that age or numbers are important, but I was curious. Our plan was to spend our time together, day and night, in the high mountains of Dharamsala, where we would intensively practice meditation in the perfect oxygenated air. This was a first for me, as I usually travel alone. We did beautiful tratak training, gazing into the snow-peaked mountains. There were lots of nature walks and trekking, some pranayama and chanting. As a practitioner, you are always in a state of mindfulness, which is easy to do in the mountains. We were in a solitary place, isolated from the public, so we could be in a constant state of mindfulness. But in a situation like that things could go very wrong, too.

Our time together in the mountains of Dharamsala was a revealing and insightful time for me, anyhow. For me, the trip was about what we could teach and learn from each other – what sort of progress would come out of it. The connection and overall understanding between my fellow yogi and me was good, so I was looking forward to what would grow out of this time together. I am used to being around students, which means teaching and lecturing, but now here we were – two yogis who were on a par with each other. What was this time going to be like? It was tantalizing to even think about it. And maybe we would have a healthy debate or two about spirituality or world philosophies.

What I learned about myself on this trip was that I had gained an even more immense love, admiration, faith and trust in the Infinite Divine Supreme. I felt balanced sharing the time with a yogi. It was an insightful way to spend the time, and we gained new ways of thinking from each other. Something valuable can always be learned when your mind is open. I never felt undermined, and I don't think he did, either.

A DIFFERENT KIND OF TRAVEL

Ganesh Ji came into my ajna chakra space! It happened this evening when I was going to bed – just like that! I wasn't doing any meditating or anything … he just came. Ganesh Ji came in beautiful red tones like a lovely murti at my ajna chakra. I didn't have much of a reaction to it other than gratitude for unexpectedly appearing to me as such a pleasant surprise. After a few seconds, the red tones in which the image first appeared gently faded away. It was just as lovely an exit as an entrance, almost like a beautiful Muslim woman saying "Salaam", with the hand gesture and all. According to Hindu belief, Ganesh is the remover of obstacles. I have never personally seen Ganesh Ji ("Ji" means "respected one"), but I believe there is some power in his existence at the level of the vastness of space and of the cosmos. "Mano ya na mano" – that's Hindi for "believe it or not".

On the morning of 6 July, I came downstairs, but my routine was a little different that day. I felt the desire to put some fresh flowers in front of the Ganesh murti that sits at my front door entrance. I have never done that before! It was just something I felt the urge to do that morning for the first time. As I was doing it, I was not yet conscious of Ganesh Ji's appearance to me. It was still sitting in my subconscious. It was only after placing the flowers at Ganesh Ji's feet that I smiled and realized that Ganesh Ji had come into my ajna chakra the night before and inspired me to place the flowers the next day.

A gentleman once asked me a question that many have asked before: "What kind of yoga do you teach?" I said, "Breath Yoga. That's the name I chose many years ago." I started explaining that all yoga requires us to be aware of our breath. He was happy to receive my explanation, and it made sense to him.

It has always been clear to me why I chose that name. I took the beautiful practice of Hat Yog developed by Saint Patanjali, the founder of yoga, and I brought to it my own style of Breath Yoga.

I give credit to the splendid universe, to the Infinite, the Divine Soul, the Supreme, for making me speak the right words when the gentleman asked me which yoga I taught. I don't know where the words came from, but for the first time, I was able to clearly explain Breath Yoga. Lately, I have been asking the Magnificent, the ever Radiant Light to please make my speech clear, to please make my words eloquent, and to make sure that the right words come out of my mouth – words that are studious, that don't make me look foolish ... Allow me to speak *your* words.

As I laid down my head to sleep, there was an explosion of stars at my ajna chakra! Dancing and shimmering, thousands of delicate stars appeared at my third eye chakra and a little above it! They sparkled like diamonds moving in synchronization, one after the other. What a sight!

The owls sing at night

The owls sing at night.
The shores roar.
Silence is heard
by the awakened souls.
I, too, tune in.

Ocean drops

Ocean drops,
I open my mouth.
I take them in
to find a whole slew
of oceans.

Today I started my meditation based on my Mayan reading. I am a Yellow Overtone Warrior. The parentals left this morning for their holiday, so I was looking forward to some alone time to address my central axis, my spine, and to allow me to return to the stars, where I come from, and to take me back to the no-time no-space cosmic consciousness. I, like many others today, am a voice for the Divine Light, a conduit, a galactic guide. And eventually I will come to the point where I will be ready to share with all people my knowledge of Cosmic Consciousness and how to reach it.

Today, in my first morning sit-down meditation, I saw a lot of light around me – there was a moment of no space. I could see myself sitting from a distance. I saw the red serpent coming out of its sleep, like it was doing a big stretch after waking up. It was not a new feeling but something that had always been there.

In my second sitting meditation early this afternoon, I felt my spine getting cold. It was a nice feeling. I saw a bird for half a second, and then I saw some lovely full flowers in a planter. As I thought of the parentals and how some of their attitudes can be an obstacle of negative energy for me, the flowers in the planter shook hard and shrank in no time – a good validation of what I need less of. I ask for the Truth and the Supreme Light to keep injecting itself deep into my nadis and to validate my real light.

I was in bed, getting ready to go to sleep, when I decided to put on some Naat Muslim spiritual music before falling asleep. I was really enjoying it, when I caught myself doing something unusual as I was returning to ordinary consciousness, and when I realized what I was doing, it made me chuckle. My hand had taken the shape of a serpent and was moving like a serpent in response to the music of the Naat. This was done unconsciously – it was my kundalini telling me it had risen and was awake! I smiled and peacefully went to sleep.

That same night, I felt a negative energy trying to enter the area around my first and second chakras. I suddenly awoke when I felt it trying to penetrate deep into me, and I immediately caught it and tossed it out so fast that it seemed shameful and foolish to even try anything with me.

I am practising intensively these days, with the guidance of a spiritual colleague, to heighten my awareness of the astral plane. This evening, I had a distance meditation experience. The experience was immediate. I felt a rush of heat in my lower body around my sacral chakra and legs. It felt like the person I was meditating with was breathing heat on me. It was not a sexual interaction, but in some way it aroused a sexual desire in me. I could feel the presence of energy through the heat, and I felt that the concentration of heat was more around my sacral chakra, and that was arousing an increasingly intense sexual desire. I turned my attention to my astral guru. I still don't know who my astral guru is – not yet, anyhow. Anyway, I asked my astral guru to make love to me, and the gods Krishna and Shiva appeared and started to make love to me – Krishna and Shiva both came to me.

The kind of love that I experienced through each of them was different. Krishna's love was gentle, with a lot of tight embracing hugs. He showered a soft love upon me. I felt secure in that kind of love. Shiva's love was dynamic – it was aggressive and explosive, yet passionate. I needed and wanted that, too. As I lay on my bed, the sensations of heat were still there – they never diminished. The love between me and Krishna and me and Shiva was simultaneous and ongoing. I kept alternating between my two beautiful lovers. At some point, the love came to an end, and I felt my body start to cool down.

Through all this, I also experienced a female figure who came to me. She was wearing all white, like a flowing white gown, but she didn't have a face, so I don't know who she was. I do know, though, that she was beautiful. Also, when she started talking, her voice was a deep, confident female voice. I don't know what she was saying, but there was a joyful, cheerful tone in her voice. I was falling asleep at that point but woke again because I kept hearing her voice. This experience lasted a few moments. All together, the whole experience was about twenty minutes. I went to bed very much in a state of peace, joy and ultimate bliss.

When I woke up this morning, I was feeling good from the previous night's meditation. I stepped into the bathroom, took off my clothes to hop in the shower, and found a love bite on my upper left breast. I was only puzzled for a moment, as I soon realized that the gods, and maybe my astral guru, too, had all made love to me last night. They left me with their precious love marks on the fair-skinned physical body I am in. I was in complete bliss and remain so still. I am in a state of full devotion to them in my physical form. I am theirs – I belong to the great energies that have presented themselves to me. The astral plane is calling, and I am going. I will always be theirs first. For all eternity, for infinity, I am theirs. I know and realize that I am one with them. I am them, and they are me – we are One.

Today I went with a couple of my girlfriends to an open house for a new yoga studio. The gals I was with are also healers and yoga teachers. We walked into the studio, and there was an abundance of shakti … lots of females – in fact, only females. So we started to make our way around the room in order to get comfortable and get to know each of the women. The three of us separated and did our own thing.

I smiled and made light conversation with a few of the women, while observing them at the same time. I gravitated towards the ones that I felt had good energy and a special spark about them. I also did some networking with the owner of the yoga studio. It turned out that she had been to India many times and wanted to do some retreats there, so we talked a bit of business, and afterwards I carried on mingling throughout the room. Since it was an open house, people were coming and going.

One woman who walked in during the open house particularly caught my eye. I knew there was something unique about her – she had an angelic appearance. We had been told that there would be a psychic reader coming, and I immediately knew it was her. I told one of the gals I was with, "Hey, that's the psychic reader over there. Go talk to her." My girlfriend wanted to have a reading done, so she was happy to know that she had arrived.

Every single one of the women in the room – about fifteen to twenty of them – all put their names on the list to have a reading done by this beautiful angelic being. One after another, the women raved about her, both the ones who had had a reading done by her before and the first-timers who came out of the psychic reading room, in awe of the insightful information she gave them about their lives. The gals I came with also came out of the room satisfied with her accurate, enlightening readings.

I was the only one who didn't put my name on the list to have a reading done. I thought to myself, "I must meet this angelic being that everyone's raving about", though not necessarily for a reading. But I was curious about what she might have to say about me, so I guess I was going for a reading after all. I already knew about myself. I just wanted to hear her take on me. With this thought, I quickly got up before it was too late and put my name on the list. My turn was taking a long time to come, so I thought perhaps she hadn't realized that I had put my name down. I waited another fifteen to twenty minutes, when she finally came out, looked at the list and called me in.

We sat down on two chairs that had been set up to face each other. The ambience quickly intensified. It was quiet for a few moments. She spoke first and said, "I just had a little treatment done in the other room, so we'll see what I channel. Let's see how this goes." She wasn't feeling too confident in herself. I didn't speak at all – no response came out of me when she said this. Then she took a moment to channel and said, "Okay, you're very confident, but your ego sometimes gets in the way of that, and you can be a bit shy." Her tone was a bit off – not as nice as I knew it could be, and she did not make eye contact with me as she was telling me this. That was my fault – I was not allowing her to relax. I smiled and softened up my energies to give us a fair chance of exchange. I needed to soften my energy to give her the respect she deserved and to allow her to channel whatever came. Now she was flowing. She took a moment to channel again. The ambience again became intense and stayed that way throughout the whole exchange, but it got more comfortable as we got more comfortable and familiar with each other.

Then she said to me, "You are in a deep study of some kind that will last a year or two, and when that study is over, you'll be gone." She had a look of confusion and disbelief on her face, almost as though she couldn't believe something that was being channelled to her. I felt strong vibrations coming from her as things got more intense in that moment. She knew I could feel her vibrations, and that made things even more confusing for her. I agreed with what she said, but I didn't say much because I wanted to see what else she would tell me.

Then she asked, "Can you tell me what you are studying?" I took a moment and then said, "I do what you do. You and I are the same. I am perfecting my inner guide and connecting with my spirituality in higher realms." That made sense to her in relation to the messages she was channelling. I added, "Yes, I will be gone." As we opened up to each other, she knew that "gone" meant to realms higher than this plane. She said, "Yes, I am getting a channelled message that you will be a master of this world and will awaken people. It will be like a pilgrimage for you, and people will follow you." I simply bowed my head and said, "Yes."

Now we were just two angelic gals hanging out. I told her I didn't care much for a reading, and she finished the sentence for me: "Yeah, I get it, you just wanted to hang." We smiled. We knew now that we understood each other, and we chatted for the next twenty minutes or so. It was a beautiful, magical, heartfelt exchange. As we parted, she said, "Good for you, girl! All the best to you!" And in the utmost humble manner, she bowed to me with her hands in a gesture of namaste. I did the same back to her. Soon afterwards, as I was making my way out to finally leave the grounds, we exchanged strong glances and sent each other flying kisses.

2012
Chakra meditation

I am lying in my bed as I feel the energy arrive. I am practicing this with my peer who is non-local and in his own home. I allow the energy to fully channel through me. I take what is offered me. It feels cool, breezy and light, like I'm floating. There is a coolness all around me, from my head to my toes and back. I feel a sense of lightness within and around me. I also am very much in tune with his sensitivity. He is letting me know he has a sensitive side, and I am receiving it. I engulf him with my compassion, channelling back to him and being compassionate towards his sensitivities.

What my peer doesn't know is that my handsome neighbour is texting me at the same time. I don't ignore the text but respond back to him. I am testing my multitasking abilities by being very much involved in a local conversation on this plane while also performing a channelling meditation and connecting to astral realms. It's great – I'm having a ball with it. The experience turns into something light, fun and airy. I finish the meditation – it only lasts fifteen minutes or so – and I continue texting with my handsome neighbour. The texting turns into subtle flirting, and we both wonder whether it wouldn't be interesting if we both acted like free spirits and got together.

Well, we did not get together and go the whole nine yards, but we did do something that was full of excitement and risk and brought back our youth again. We each stepped out of our respective homes at 1 a.m. to meet in our driveways. We both smiled and thought, "This is crazy, but it's a good crazy." So we went back into his garage and had a late-night kiss. It was a bit off at first because of the feeling of risk – that feeling of, "OMG, I hope we don't get caught!" But we finally got caught up in the passion of it all. It lasted a good few minutes until I ran out of the garage, saying, "Okay, bye – see ya."

We'll see when the next rendezvous will be – or even if it will be. Sometimes a spontaneous moment is just what you need in life, a one-time thing that makes it ever so memorable. I was so high that night! First my breezy, floating meditation, and then my crazy late-night rendezvous. What a life this is – full of color! Just embrace it … be in the moment, have some fun, take some risks, play a little …

I have always done chakra meditation. But it was the intense regular practice of connecting non-locally with my spiritual peer that allowed for full-throttle cosmic travels. And that brought on all kinds of new perceptions and sensations during my day-to-day waking hours.

I carried on doing what I did during the week – teaching classes, working on programs, etc. But I was starting to feel a change taking place. Day by day, moment by moment, I was noticing differences in my perception, my actions, my voice – everything was different, and it was good.

For example, I stepped out to run some errands, and I double-checked myself to make sure I was wearing clothes. I glanced downwards: "Oh yes, I have them on." That made me send out a question to the astral plane: "Why I am doing this?" The answer came back that I was shedding my old skin to become the real me, the person I was supposed to be. I was also noticing that my aura of universal love had immense presence now. My heart chakra was touching the continents. It was going around the globe to all nations, all people, all faiths, including non-believers – every person, every animal, every planet, galaxy and star. My sense of universal love had become omnipresent and powerful.

At first, it was like a ringing in my ears – not an annoying ringing but a sound that I wanted to hang out with for as long as I could. It was subtle and soothing. It felt right, like something right was going on or beginning. I also heard my spiritual colleague ask the angels to help him help me. I heard him say, "Let her in – she's okay. Let her come in." I also felt a presence near my right hand. It didn't last too long, but the ringing itself wouldn't go away, which was okay because I was fully enjoying it. I remained within the sound of the ringing. I could also here some laughter and giggles, like shy little girls having a good time.

The next day, first thing in the morning, I kept hearing the same laughter and giggles coming from above. I was down here laughing with them. I woke up with a feeling of real joy and bliss. I even did a little angel dance, with my arms in the air like I was flying and skipping. It was so joyful – it's hard to find the words to describe it. All day long the giggles and laughter rang in my ears. A lovely experience! I did start questioning it, though: "Is this all they do – laugh and giggle? Do they ever sound like adults?" To me, it sounded like little shy girls having a ball. Nothing wrong with that, but I was keen to hear them express a different character.

I didn't feel much during my meditation this time. My peer and I were doing the meditation together non-locally. What I did feel was his hand, his energies working over my entire body from head to toe. It felt like he was doing a full-body scan of all my chakras. I felt him smile and say, "She's doing good – real good." At one point, I also felt his hand go over my thigh. This alerted me, and I questioned it, thinking, "Why is he going over my thigh?" But I embraced the feeling. Within the next couple of days, I noticed red marks on my thighs in the same spot where I had felt his energies working. Amazing.

During the meditation, I had been kind of dozing off because I was tired. Then a cute little blonde girl with two pigtails appeared before my eyes. She was pleasant to look at. She was smiling at me with her very beautiful, bright blue eyes. She stayed for a good few moments. It was nice – I enjoyed that she presented herself to me.

Wow! What can I say? Ask and you shall receive. I asked, and I got. As soon as the meditation started, a very confident adult female voice started talking to me. She said hello, and I said hello. She had a subtle smile. This time I didn't hear any giggling – no shy girls. It was just me and this woman. We connected well. I realized that she was the one who would be speaking to me when I needed to help others. She was my guardian angel. I asked her, "Are you the one who will be speaking to me all the time? Are you the one who will be speaking to me when I need to help others?" Both her answers were a very confident "Yes". Then I said to her, "I love you, I love you, I love you." She laughed and said, "I love you, too." We also had our moments of silence, which were just as beautiful. She knew I was taking all of this in.

I said to her, "Where have the giggling girls gone?" She said, "They're here." And then I heard them above her doing their usual thing. I got emotional at one point and asked her, "Is this really real, or am I just getting emotional for no reason? Are you really here? Are you really talking to me?" She said, "Yes, it's real." I knew we were together now, so with that comfort, I said "Bye", and she said "Goodnight". So we stayed together for some time. I didn't want to let her go, but then I did.

After that, I got on Skype with my peer to share my experience with him, and I got all emotional and started crying. He told me "It's okay." I answered, "I know, but I just can't believe it." While we were on Skype, he said, "See if you can call her back, and ask her to take you to their astral realm." So I did, and she came back faster than the speed of light. She said, "You've already been here." I smiled, nodded my head, and thought to myself, "That's right – I have." I got back on Skype with my friend and said, "I've already been there." I started describing it to him. It was by Shiv Lok – close to that. He smiled big and said, "Yes, that sounds right. The angelic realm ends right where Shiv Lok starts." Then he said, "So you've been to Shiv Lok, too, huh? I didn't think you would get there that fast." I said, "Well, actually, I've been above Shiv Lok as well."

I was sitting in meditation a couple of days ago on 26 September 2012, and I tried to go high and deep. And that was what I got – I went to Shiv Lok and above it. While I was in Shiv Lok, I asked to go higher, and I went. That's where Krishna and Jesus sit. I asked Krishna and Jesus, "How come you guys are presenting yourselves to me in physical form when I know that you are energy? I know that you've walked the earth and that you took physical form on the earth plane.

I know that the Shiv Lok where you are has no physical form because Shiva did not manifest on earth, so why would he show himself in a physical form? It makes sense to me that I see only energy in Shiv Lok. But in your own realm, I see you physically manifested." So Krishna and Jesus said to me, "We have shown you our manifested physical forms to let you know you have found us, that you have reached us." Then Jesus put his hand on top of my head and gave me his blessing. I said, "Yes, I understand." I was telling all this to my friend, and he was overwhelmed – he had no words.

All this has come to me within the last few days. Things are changing so rapidly day by day that it's almost too hard for me to keep up.

2 October 2012
Hello, Angels

Today, I said a small prayer for a few minutes before my meditation. I prayed to Durga Mata, who is an Indian goddess. Durga Mata was the first experience I'd ever had of spirituality. It happened when I was sixteen years old, when I went to Vaishnu Devi with my parents. I will never forget the pull it had on me. I was totally affected by her rapture. So I wanted to pay her my respects.

My meditation was very, very peaceful. I went up higher into the angelic realm near Shiv Lok. I saw a cloud with a silver lining. My friend says I went even higher into the angelic realm than I thought, and that's why it felt so peaceful. The silver cloud is the high point of the angelic realm.

It was ever so peaceful a feeling – it was a feeling of complete silence and stillness. And in that stillness, I saw before me a vision of a tiger's face, roaring and breathing intensely. It was so intense that I could not ignore it. It startled me for a moment, but I realized that it was Durga Mata and her tiger, and that she was giving me her blessing. She sits on a tiger, and that's what I saw! I quickly accepted the many blessings from Durga Mata and her beautiful tiger! I prayed to her, and she acknowledged my prayer! Now I am just waiting for the true angelic channelling to begin – the connection between Heaven and Earth that will help people and give them the messages and answers they are meant to hear.

After all my meditations and connections with the angelic realm and beyond, I am noticing the physiological changes in my body very intensely. As I sit still, my body constantly shakes and moves from side to side, but the movement is so subtle that nobody would know it was happening. I understand that what's at work is the expansion of my prana and auras as they do their thing. They are letting me know every second that I have expanded beyond my body and that my presence is very much connected to other realms at all times!

I went into the backyard to see how my beautiful red feather was doing amidst the other real flowers. It was still there, showing its valor. Even better, there was another baby feather growing out of the same root and plant. Amazing! Feathers growing in my backyard … thank you for the blessings, Krishna!

It's Saturday, and I'm at a healing centre to do a healing session for one of my female clients. Our session ends, and I realize again today how my human makeup is changing physiologically after all these enlightened experiences, channellings, and connections to new realms.

As we were getting ready to leave the centre, someone needed to quickly go pee. I waited for the person to finish up in the bathroom, and as my senses became heightened, I immediately smelt the urine. It was an amazing, unbelievable experience. I had such a strong presence of mind about what she was doing in there that my senses connected to her action, and I could smell it. It's fascinating what you can tune into when your being expands beyond the merely physical.

Since the feather blessing from Krishna, nothing phenomenal like that has happened to me, but in my yoga studio, I did notice a puddle of salt water on the shelf, right beside my salt lamp. I wondered just for a second about this saltwater puddle, but then I quickly made sense of it and smiled as I thought, "As usual – this is my life." This is the shelf where I place the money when people pay me. And it's also the shelf where I keep the salt lamp that I turn on to ward off any bad energies that might be entering into my studio. So I said to the salt lamp, "Thank you for blessing the monetary funds that I place next to you when they come to me. And thanks for warding off negative energies in order to protect me." It's consciousness at work. The salt lamp is letting me know, "I'm working with you, doing my job warding off bad energies and blessing the monetary fruits that come to you."

The salt lamp and I are officially friends now! We are advaita – there is no duality between us. I mean, I could be wrong, but considering the pattern of my life, with all its spiritual phenomena, you can see why I'm going there with this one, too. I talk to the things around me, and they talk back to me. I hear and feel their energy vibrating with mine. I feel the life in all things – a plant, a table, my books, the salt lamp and the space around me. Nothing is without life – it's all-pervading. I speak to the space in front of me, and it speaks back to me. It's not empty but filled with spirit energy and life. There is no difference between me and the things around me. Everything is meshed and one. Everything is me, and I am all that is.

It's still 13 October, the same day as the one on which the salt lamp blessings happened. What a great Saturday today has been! In the daytime, there was the salt lamp blessing, followed by an evening of angelic blessings. That evening, I went to my cousin's sister's family party. Not much for me to do there, but I was a good sport about it, mingling and making small talk, etc. My cousin's brother was there, and we got on great. He's an astrologer, so we always have lots to talk about. He did my reading about five years ago, in 2007. He said he found my chart to be very unique. The chart said that I would be doing some astral travelling … well, well, isn't that interesting? Because that's exactly what I was doing in September 2012.

Life is moving so quickly with my journeys to other realms. There are no words to express the love and gratitude I feel for this. I love it – and now I'm also starting to get comfortable with it. It's where I belong. It's where I come from, so now I am finally connecting to my real home. Today at the party, I told people that I did angelic readings. I have never handed out so many business cards as I did in one hour this evening.

I even did an unexpected reading while I was there. There were two sisters there who had lost their mother a couple of years back. Immediately, the mother came to me, and I passed her messages on to her daughters. It was the first time I had spoken with a deceased soul, so now I knew that I could do this, too! I'm learning that people can get quite emotional when I tell them things, and I completely understand this. I just have to get used to it – actually, I think I already am. I handled it okay. It was an amazing connection for me. The experience felt very natural.

I also did one other reading. This question was for the angels. It was a common question asked by a girl who wanted to know whether she was going to have babies soon. I think I answered her appropriately. It wasn't the answer she wanted to hear, but I told her what I heard. I also did a couple of quick chakra scans and readings – just like that. It was a great evening for me – not what I thought it would be, a boring family gathering. Instead, it ended up being a really stimulating time for me.

Being on a roll from last night, I've kept that momentum going. This is what I do – this is my calling! Today I had my yoga students at the house for practice. After practice, I let them know about my connection with other realms. Some of them mentioned a grandparent they'd lost. I told them some simple things I was seeing about it. One of the gals got quite emotional. I guess I should expect this to happen when I give readings. I'm learning that more and more. I'm coming to understand it now.

Sunday night I was going to bed, and I could feel the space in front of me shaking – and it was! I am always jolted by these experiences … just for a few moments, but I am definitely aware of them when they happen. I am also continuing to experience many physiological changes on a daily basis.

I am in a state of just being. I'm a modern yogi. Sometime way back when, I knew I had to change. I knew I had to bring some kind of growth to my life, and growth meant change. I made the changes slowly but surely, and now I am immersed in change. I just do it. I *am* change … because nothing is permanent.

Recently, I was watching the news, and they were saying that people would soon not only be going to outer space but staying there. They will be leaving the planet Earth and living in space! It was not that many years ago that men first walked on the moon, and now it will be possible for them to live there. And they say it will happen sooner rather than later! It all makes a lot of sense to me, as we are coming into the Golden Age, the age of spirituality and higher thinking, that people will have a choice of whether to stay here or go. When it comes to spirituality, that refers more to interdimensional travel, but advanced space travel can be viewed as a symbol of that.

On finishing my meditation today, I gave a flying kiss gesture to the skies. I do this sometimes to show my everlasting love and gratitude. But today, as I was finishing, I felt a very cool breeze, a strong energy presence by my right cheek, close to the corner of my right lip. I was receiving a kiss back from the Supreme Energies. I smiled and said, "Thank you".

The more I delve into my spiritual being, the less I feel the need to be surrounded by crowds of people. I also don't feel the need to address relatives as "Aunt Jenny" or "Uncle Joe". To me, everyone is the same, so I would rather just say "Jenny" or "Joe". I have no particular attachment to my relatives, so addressing everyone by his or her first name seems fair and neutral. They say that this is the case when a yogi truly becomes a yogi – this is one of the obstacles they face. Family relationships start to fade away, and everyone who was once seen as family is now seen as being equal to the rest of the world.

As I was going to bed, I saw one of my childhood friends. Her feet were just slightly wet with blood and water combined. When I saw the water with the blood, it made it okay in my thoughts.

When I went to bed tonight, I saw my father's ghost. My father is still alive, but I saw his ghost, anyway. It was just his face, which appeared with a calm, warm smile. I acknowledged it and dozed off.

This is a very normal experience for some of us. I'm sure I have mentioned that we are all energies and subtle energies. We all have a subtle body. So if you see your buddy's or family member's ghost, you are just experiencing them in subtle-body form. It's kinda neat – enjoy it.

Last year, 2012, was a compelling year for me. I have tightly bonded with and rooted myself in the Divine Light. My love bond with the Divine Light is unbreakable, unshakable, and forever in bloom. This Supreme Light has won my love over and over again. I love no other as I love the Supreme Divine Light. We are One now. We reach out to each other every second of every waking hour and even in deep sleep. The Divine Light and I have found each other. We belong together. They – all Supreme Lights – need me, just as I need them. I am fully aware that the Divine Light needs my love, and I give it unconditionally. I am meant for God, as God is meant for me. We are One!! We grow together. For each other. Forever. Amen.

I had been a vegetarian since May 2012. Even before that, I was not a big non-vegetarian. But in May 2012, I cut out all poultry, fish, and eggs. Then, in December 2012, I started having non-vegetarian cravings again, after a long seven months. That was the month I went to the grocery store, stood in front of the sandwich meats counter and did it. I asked the girl to slice me just a few pieces of turkey – not more than a few. She handed them over to me with a smile. I'm sure she must have wondered: "Just a few slices?" Anyhow, I ate them, and it was fine. No problem. I did not have any guilt feelings or unhealthy reactions. It was just like any other healthy food I ate. Well, sliced meat is really not that healthy. It's full of nitrates. But the occasional deli meat is all right. Anyhow, it got me thinking about eating a non-vegetarian diet again. I didn't act on it until the New Year, though – until 11 January 2013. It was a weekend when I confidently announced at home: "Let's have fish today." The look on my father's face was: "Are you serious?" I replied, "Yes, I am." And that was it. After seven months, I broke my vegetarian diet and had non-vegetarian food. And it was fine. I enjoyed it. There really wasn't much to think about.

When I went to bed that evening, I asked my angels and Divine Lights, "Is this okay? It's not going to affect the beautiful connection, the spiritual bond I have made with you?" I got my answers, and then some. The next morning, I woke up so inspired by my Divine Lights. Without a cup of tea or anything, I got out my laptop and starting writing away about another enlightened insight for my book *A Modern Yogi*.

Each day I feel more and more connected to the divine energies. I feel their presence within me each day through some heightened experience or another.

I was corresponding with my editor via email. She asked me to put in some hard prayers for our book, prayers that I would get to meet the publisher she had in mind for us – that I should meet him properly. When I went to bed that evening, I centred all my attention on the publisher. I got a faint trace of his cologne or some scent he wears. I could also hear his voice, his laughter. I saw him gathering with others to have some kind of meeting. He was wearing dark colours. I also got a sweet scent from my editor – some sweet scent that she wears. What this tells me is that each day I am becoming more and more conscious of being connected on a non–local level to the people I will eventually be meeting and working with. I thank the Divine Lights for this blessing, this gift.

I know and see when people love God, when they are passionate about it. No human is capable of the dreams and wishes and joy that the Divine Lights can give. Each day I am in complete awe of these illuminated, ever so radiant energies that shine their love on me and prove to me every day that they can make anything happen.

The same night that I experienced the faint scents, when I lay my head down to sleep, I saw radiant silver and white clouds – just a few of them. They would pop up and then gently fade away.

I have a loyal student and client. Let's call him "The Seeker". He enjoys participating in the meditation programs I do, and he is open to all kinds of paths that lead to spiritual growth. He does ayahuasca every so often, and he shares his experiences with me. I have been in his journeys. When he travels in this way, he says that a female spirit comes to him and guides him on the journey. He gets to see the people in his life, and he has told me a couple of times that I, too, have been in those experiences that the female spirit has shown him. The first time he told me this, I didn't know how to react or what to say. I was amazed at how our spirits all connect. I was amazed to hear how this female spirit led him to me. The Seeker told me that the reason she led him to me on their astral journey was that I could help heal him. She told him that he should continue to come to my classes. I was deeply moved when I heard this. I felt honoured that she had led him to me.

More recently, he explained to me that the female spirit had again led him to me. She keeps leading him to me. She tells him that I can help him. When he told me that this time, something came over me, and I felt her presence very strongly nearby. Tears started rolling down my face. I felt so much gratitude that this female spirit's trust in me was so real and so faithful. The Seeker and I weren't even sitting in front of each other when he shared it with me – he told me this through a text message. So much emotion came over me in a matter of seconds. It happened, first of all, because of this lovely female spirit, to whom I now feel very connected. She is a very strong and outspoken shakti spirit. I feel her. I am so honoured and grateful for being allowed to sense her strong presence and to feel the connection between us.

Next, I have immense gratitude for God, for the Divine Lights that have given me the gift of healing others, like the Seeker, who reach out for my help and my love. I feel overwhelmed with gratitude that the Divine Lights have called me to help others. Life is so spirited! I am thankful for what the Divine Lights are showing me and allowing me to feel and experience each day. Every day, they are showing me a life that is more and more spiritual.

My friend the Seeker goes on his ayahuasca journeys every day. They're led by his trusted shaman. I appear a lot in his travels. I did some healing on the Seeker recently. My methods of healing are not taught by anyone. I just do what I'm told by the Divine messages. They lead my hands around like dancing tentacles. I had to pull. I had to pull stuff out of the Seeker. I pulled like I was actually pulling a big, heavy, thick rope. I just kept going. It was never-ending. When I finished the healing session, I told him I had pulled stuff out of his back. He told me that when he was doing his ayahuasca travelling, he travelled far and deep, and it was all led by his shaman. He said I was there a lot, pulling and pulling just like I was actually doing to him the day he was here. He said to his spirit guide in his travels, "Hey, that's the same pulling Reyna was doing to me in person." And then he started doing the same thing. He was perhaps guided by me and his spirit guide to pull – to just pull stuff out of people to bring healing to them.

I personally have never done any ayahuasca ceremonies, but I feel connected to the practice, thanks to my introduction to it by the Seeker. Ayahuasca feels me, and I feel it. We're all connected outside of this realm – far, far away from this material plane, deep within our DNA and beyond that DNA ... What's beyond our DNA, anyhow? Have you ever wondered?

Every now and then when I'm doing an angelic reading, someone will ask me, "Reyna, can you see my past lives?" The first time I was asked this question I was quick to say, "No, I cannot." I was naive to react this way. Perhaps I can see their past lives. I'm not sure yet. I know I can see my own past lives. The question of past lives is an important enough question to collect some answers, considering that I'm an energy worker. I have to be open and see what kind of channellings come to me. After all, I am clairvoyant enough to be able to see what they cannot. I say this with great humility.

Lately, I have been tuning into who I was before this lifetime. Was I always raised as a Hindu? Did I live in different time periods? How many different people have I been? Was I always female, or was I sometimes male? I have received most of the answers to my questions. However, my search continues every day. Once you get a taste of knowing who you were in your past lives, it's hard to let go. You want to know more and more of the details of your past being. And that's okay. You will have much more clarity about your life today. But it's important to not obsess about your past. After all, it is your past, so really be and live in the present.

I was never really of this earth realm, but I have had many lifetimes in a physical body, each time to do spiritual work. I still had many lessons to learn, so I had to keep coming back to this planet. This is my final time on earth, but it's not my final destination. I will go back to where I belong in the astral realm once my work is done here. I have to spread the word of love from God(s). I have to help people learn to look from within. I have to open their hearts to things that they might find shocking to hear or accept. But what I say all comes down to *great love*, big love!

Knowing your past lives can be a major healing experience, as it can have significant connections to your present life. I have the ability to heal people in two ways. The first is by seeing and feeling their energies. I get a feel, a vibe of their chakras or what I call chakra readings, and then I get them to unblock their chakras by doing chakra meditation with them. I get them on their way to ultimately discovering their own chakras and continuing to heal themselves. The second way is through my astral connection to the spiritual – to the angels, guides, masters and God(s). They speak to me. I'm just the voice that conveys the message. I can see that people are desperately looking for answers in their lives, and I'm happy to convey the messages that will help them. I call this angelic reading or angelic connection.

I pray for all people that they understand that what I tell them comes not from me but from a much higher place, a spiritual realm. That realm channels it to me, and I then say it to the world. This is not an option for me. It's a fact I have to accept. I must speak the words that I hear coming from high above. It is my duty to represent the Holy Light(s). I am honored that they have chosen me to do this work. I never would have guessed it, but at the same time, now that I know about my past lives, I am clear that this is my purpose. I no longer fear delving into my own past lives or attempting to do so for others. I am happy to channel the messages that constantly come to me from the other side.

When you're meant to do something, all the signs start to appear in your life. It was my angel guides that led me to be open to seeing my own past lives. So seeing people's past lives may be possible for me. I guess I'll find out some day. As a channel, I have recognized that it's not under my control. You never know what is going to happen when you do a reading for someone. Maybe you will see the person's past lives, and maybe not. It's truly fascinating stuff. But I must keep my channel open at all times. Whatever I am meant to receive is what is read.

Through the gift of God(s), I have been able to see the light from within and feel the spiritual presence. I can channel and connect with the astral realm through my chakras, which are open and aligned. My goal is to get you there, too. My chakras have been open for quite some time, and I am always thankful for this gift. The astral connection to spirit – to angels, guides, masters and God(s) – is somewhat new. I'm handling it with great pride. I'm honoured to have such a position, but at the same time it's a big job. No slacking on this one.

I thank God I have a purpose and a skill here. I started thinking that maybe I had absolutely no skills in this world. I have a skill, though. It's just not of this world. That's why I have found adapting to other people and to this life on earth very challenging – everything from my school days to getting into the work force to relationships. I'm getting better. The spiritual angels, guides and masters tell me all the time that they had to put me down here on earth to be a messenger. So I'm doing the best I can to make sure I follow through with that. My *soul* purpose is to please God(s). And I have a very pure intention to do so.

MIAMI SURPRISES

Hmmm … what can I say about this trip? It definitely was not what you would expect of South Beach, Miami. But with the way my life goes, it fit perfectly. A few months earlier, I'd done a remote reading for a young lady in her early thirties who lives in NYC. By "remote", I mean that I communicated the channelling through Skype. We never met in person. She was pleased with the reading and stayed in touch with me via internet.

Sometime around March, I started thinking about a small get-away, a little trip I could go on. I asked my NYC client about Costa Rica, since she had mentioned being there, and I thought it might be a cool place to check out. Then she said, "Hey, I'm gonna be in Miami in April. Why don't you join me there?" I said, "Really? Are you sure? 'Cause I'm serious about going on a little get-away, and if you really mean it – sure, I'd be happy to join you." She said, "Oh, yes, yes! Please join me! I would love to have you." It was a done deal. I booked my flight from Toronto to Miami to meet with a girl I had never met in person before – a remote client! Those who know me, though, know that I am spontaneous enough to do stuff like this.

I didn't hear from her much during the final days leading up to the trip. It struck me as kind of odd. I had a questioning sense about it, but then I brushed it off and thought, "Well, she's from New York, and New Yorkers are always on the go – busy busy busy." I reached out to her again via text but got no reply.

I started packing the night before, and while I was doing so, I experienced a very pure moment, in which I connected to the spiritual realm and thought, "I have a feeling this trip to Miami is just going to be you and me." Then I repeated it, because I realized that my inner words were speaking the truth: "It's going to be just you and me in Miami." I continued packing with a positive attitude and kept thinking, "I have no idea what Miami has in store for me. That will unravel when I get there … but I do know it's gonna be an adventure."

On my first day there, as soon as I left the airport, I again reached out to the "stranger" I was supposed to meet and hang out with. Finally, we connected: "Oh, hey, I'm here, too. I'm heading to my hotel." I said, "Yes, me too. Okay, we'll connect and meet up shortly." Then I got a text from her: "Hey, check-in is not till later. Wanna meet up for some lunch and drinks?" I texted back, "Sure! Tell me where. See you soon." That was the first and last time we saw each other on the trip we were supposed to be spending together. I saw her friend more than I saw her. The friend she flew down with, a tall, handsome Puerto Rican guy, connected with me a couple of times. I got to do a chakra and angel reading for him. It was nice for me to be doing my thing.

After the three of us had lunch that day, we separated to go to our different hotels. When evening rolled around, I still hadn't heard from her. Miami doesn't really get started until 10-ish, so I figured it was okay – we just hadn't connected yet. But I knew something wasn't right. By then, it was already after 10 p.m., so I reached out again, thinking that this was becoming kind of a nuisance. Anyway, I sent a text: "Hey, what's up? What's the plan?" The text I got back read: "???" Now I was really confused. Then I got another text: "I'm really tired. It's been a long day, and I'm in bed."

The pure spiritual words I'd spoken while packing were becoming reality. Here I was in Miami, all by myself. What should I do now? Luckily for me, I was across from the popular Delano Hotel, which has an impressive and beautiful lounge area out back, with white cabanas, tall palm trees and a pool. So off I went to the Delano. I got myself a virgin mojito and then looked for a safe and comfortable place to sit for a couple of hours. I ended up sitting down on a white leather sofa where I could console myself and feel right at home under the beautiful, tall palm trees. And I felt they needed my attention, too. The second I sat down, there was an automatic connection between me and those tall palm trees. You could say that we bowed to each other, acknowledging what was real. Nobody else was paying any attention to them. Everybody was looking across at people's heads, and nobody chose to look up at the real beauty. I finished my mojito, headed back to the hotel and called it a night.

Another day began. I didn't hear from the "stranger", but it didn't matter now. I was heading to the beach to connect with the ocean! I rented a chair, sat down and sighed with joy as I put on my tanning lotion. I thought of my guides, my Holy Lights, as I looked out at the vast ocean before me. "Yay! I'm here with you by the Atlantic Ocean. That's all we need – each other." That became my morning routine for the next couple of days on the trip.

At one point, the "stranger" reached out to me again via text: "Hey, how's it going? What have you been doing?" I texted back: "I'm doing great! I've been hanging out by the oceanside, etc." She then made sure to tell me, "Well, you know, I'm kinda busy doing fitness classes here. I'm juggling a lot, so don't wait around for me. We'll hook up later. I'm decompressing right now." I said, "Okay." There was not much left to say. Anyhow, by now her words didn't affect me much. I knew this trip was about me, myself and the magnetic pull of the sea. What more could I ask for? I was blessed.

I spent my days walking around the town, looking at the shops, observing people, going for lunch and dinner. I did a lot of walking. But I didn't care much for the shops and so on. Every day and every evening, I found myself magnetically pulled towards the sea. I was more than blissful by the ocean. I did some of my Breath Yoga by the shore, and I talked to the sea. We were one. And I also discovered the boardwalk, which was more than twelve kilometres long. It was awesome – the evening walk, with the ocean breeze hitting my face and skin as I inhaled the oxygen-rich ocean air, listened to the crashing waves and gazed at the stars above. The negative ions from the ocean were feeding me, keeping my lungs healthy. The ocean is such a healer.

Then, an interesting thing happened as I was walking around one day looking at the shops, etc. I happened to see the "stranger" laughing and enjoying herself over drinks with some friends. I just stopped. I didn't say a word but waited for her to see me standing there. What a moment! Thank you, Holy Lights. She looked up and said, "OMG, what are you doing here?" What an uncomfortable moment for all of them! I answered, "I was just walking around, hanging out. I see you're doing the same. I thought you were decompressing." She said, "Yeah, well I am. This *is* decompressing." She looked to her friends to help her out, and one guy jumped to the rescue. "Yeah well, you know, in our industry, we have to relax after all that exercise. You know, we want to just chill and relax." I said, "Yeah. Right." I knew that words weren't necessary for me to express what I was thinking. The power of the truth was enough for me right then. In that instant, I recognised the power of spiritual guidance to show us the truth. I stood there in silence for more than a few moments, and not once did she say, "Come sit down – join us." That validated my impression even more. I was being brushed off and avoided. It was a sure thing now. I smiled, silently waved good-bye, and walked away.

Within twenty minutes of that incident, a young black man approached me on Lincoln Road, South Beach's stylish pedestrian mall, and said something like, "Would you like a smile today? Here you go!" He handed me a smiley face sticker. Then he handed me a piece of literature on the ISKCON Hare Rama Hare Krishna temple in Coconut Grove. I was so pleased to meet someone spiritual! It is the rarest thing to openly find that on Lincoln Road! Lincoln Road is all about bling-bling – high-end shopping, Tesla car showrooms. Finding a Hare Krishna advocate there is rare. But once again the Holy Lights made me smile and, as always, won my heart. "This trip is so about you and me, isn't it?" My heart filled with love and gratitude towards them. There we were, this young black chap and I, talking about spirituality and its effect on our lifestyles. We introduced ourselves to each other. I told him my name was Reyna, and as we were talking, it started pouring. It was like a storm – hard, powerful rain just pouring down. It was awesome! He said, "Rain is pouring down for Reyna." We had such a great time chatting about our spiritual views. By the time we realized it, three hours had gone by.

Towards the end of our conversation, I asked him, "Do you know of some spiritual yoga centre I can go to?" He told me about Synergy on Española Way. We then said our good-byes, but before that he confessed: "I've never spoken so long to someone who isn't a vegetarian. But I'm not allowing that to impact the joy and energy I'm receiving from you." I thanked him for recognising my innate qualities and values as a spiritual being, and I explained that what I ate did not affect my love of spiritual connection. Spirit and the Holy Lights loved and accepted me as I was. In fact, they didn't expect me to change anything. I was meant to be as I was – maybe a new kind of spiritual leader, a modern-day version.

Before we parted, the young man was happy to let me put my hand on his upper back, where he needed healing. And it was a pleasure for me to do it for him. We got some strange looks, as all this was still taking place on Lincoln Road. The people walking up and down with their expensive shopping bags seemed to be thinking, "What are these two freaks up to?" I didn't do much healing on his back and suggested that this might not be the right spot. If he wanted to, he could come see me that evening between 7 and 7:30 p.m. for a proper healing. He was quite excited and said, "Yes, I'll be there!" So we finally parted ways as we looked forward to meeting again that evening.

I waited until about 8:00 and then left to go to Synergy. I figured maybe we weren't meant to meet again. Also, it was still pouring rain. "He's not showing up", I thought, so I left. When I returned to my hotel later that evening, I found out from the front desk that he had shown up just after I left. "It's okay", I thought. "We were only meant to have that special time in the rain on Lincoln Road."

Finding Synergy was an adventure in itself. One place I saw on the way had a huge painting of "Om" outside on the porch. As I moved closer, I could see more paintings dealing with subjects like Shiva, the chakras and Buddha. There was a Venezuelan man sitting right in front of me. "Hi, how are you?" He was cheerful yet calm. I said, "I'm looking for a yoga centre called Synergy. Is this it?" "No, it is not. I do spiritual paintings here, as you can see." I said, "Yes, they're beautiful." He continued: "Synergy is just up the street. You have to go past all the Spanish restaurants, and it's tucked away down a little alley. A little tricky to find, but you'll see it." I said, "Okay, thank you. I'll look for it." He said, "What do you do?" "I'm a spiritual mentor and healer. I also teach chakra meditation, so I'm looking to find a place that teaches it. I just want to spend some time there being a part of the circle I belong to and supporting my fellow spiritual practitioners." He said, "You'll like Sadhu. You must attend Sadhu's classes. He teaches Kundalini Yoga. He just got back from India – I know you'll enjoy him. He also teaches at 4 a.m. You can attend his very early morning sessions." I got quite excited and said, "Yes, I will only go to his classes. I will go and find out when he's there."

The Venezuelan guy was quite interesting, too. He had lived in India many years back, and it was there that he had become spiritually inclined. He expressed such beauty in his paintings and drawings of Shiva, the chakras, Buddha, and the Om syllable. He said that when he retired, he would settle in India, move away from material things and live more of a sadhu lifestyle. So far, that was the second spiritual experience I'd had, and it was only my second day in Miami. Life in Miami was just filled with an abundance of spirituality. It was all around me. And it was as attracted to me as I was to it.

I made it to Synergy but just missed the evening class. The young French guy working the desk told me to come back the next day, that there was a 7:30 class that Sadhu would be teaching. So I went back the next day for an evening kundalini class with Sadhu. I got there a little early, and I looked like a mess. I had been walking all day. I ended up meeting the Puerto Rican guy and one of his friends for lunch. After that, we walked around for some time. Before I knew it, it was time for me to get to the yoga centre. I didn't have time to change, so I arrived wearing my stretchy jeans that I'd been wearing all day. At least, they were stretchy. I was filling out paperwork, and my back was turned when Sadhu walked in, so I didn't see him right away, and I didn't know whether he had walked in alone or not. Oh my, here we go again! As soon as I saw him, I felt magnetically pulled towards him. I'm not sure whether it was because of his cool demeanour or his tall, handsome physique or his captivating eyes or his purity. It was probably all of it. He was wearing white clothes and a white turban. I smiled and said hello. He said hello back, and we locked eyes. If I hadn't pulled away my look, we would have stayed locked. I had to pull away, though. It was too intense. As I looked away, I noticed a young woman sitting down, simple and beautiful, also in all white with a white turban. I realized that she must have walked in with him, though I hadn't noticed. I smiled and said hello to her, too. She kindly smiled back at me. I thought, "Whew! Good thing she's smiling at me." I experienced a moment of guilt – because of the eye-locking with her partner, perhaps. I stood there for a few seconds, absorbing it all and collecting myself. Sadhu sat down on the stool next to where I was standing. I noticed the wedding band on his finger. "Darn!" I thought. But at the same time, it was okay, because really – what was I gonna do? Marry him? Probably not.

So now that everything was clear and I'd had a few seconds to collect myself, I felt capable of making conversation. I started by telling them about myself. I was just visiting Miami, and that's what led me to their centre. I wanted to do some meditation practice. I, too, was a kundalini/chakras teacher. Both of them responded with "Oh, really! Wow, that's great!" I said that I'd never done that style of Kundalini Yoga before, so I was happy to experience it. They taught the Yogi Bhajan style, while mine was the traditional kundalini chakra style. Both paths are all about the awakening of the self, so everything was great. I am always open to learning what my fellow yogis and spiritual mentors are teaching.

I did their practice for two days. The day after that I had a very early start at 4 a.m. I didn't sleep at all that night, because the previous night's class ended at around nine. As I was leaving to walk back to the hotel, I ran into my Venezuelan friend. He commented, "Looks like you're coming from Sadhu's class." "Yes", I said, "I just finished. He's wonderful! His class is wonderful, too." Then I added, "I'm going back again at 4 a.m. this morning." My Venezuelan friend had been enjoying his wine, so he was feeling good. We stood outside, just talking and talking as the time flew by. I kept thinking that I needed to get some sleep for my meditation practice at 4 a.m. But it was a beautiful night, and we were enjoying conversing with each other. Then my new Puerto Rican friend texted me. He wanted me to do a reading for him. It was good timing, actually. I was feeling good after the evening's kundalini meditation. We met and walked near the ocean, where we found a quiet spot to sit down and do the reading. It must have been after midnight when I finally got back to my hotel room. I had to shower and pack. I didn't want to leave it until the last minute. By the time I was done with everything, it was 3 a.m. Now I had to get ready to leave for the 4 a.m. meditation.

So off I went to my kundalini meditation practice. It was the best way to begin my last day in Miami. I still had a whole day in South Beach, so I embraced the opportunity to spend it by the ocean, and I did my long 12-kilometre trek on the boardwalk again. After that, I figured I deserved some shopping, so I managed to fit that in. I was enjoying just being, and I thanked my guiding Lights for the three spiritual people and experiences that had filled my time in South Beach, Miami. Three is my number.

HEAVEN AND EARTH

Why is it that whenever I wear my tiger eye necklace, it reminds me of Neil, my brother? I got my answer. He is one of my guiding lights. And tiger eye is supposed to help keep your channel open. Also, his sun sign was Leo, and the tiger and the lion are both from the cat family. But those who know me know I don't have any dependencies – at least, not most of the time. So I don't want that to happen with my tiger eye necklace, either, even though it's associated with Neil. He is around me whether I wear this pendant or not.

It's amazing how the objects in our lives will work with us when we pay attention to them and don't just see them as objects but as living energies. When we start to connect with all things as energies, we are able to see through them and speak to them as more than just objects. And the kind of energy each one manifests depends on how evolved we are in our higher perception.

One day, I was out and about, driving around, and I asked the gods, "How can I heal my lungs?" The answer came in quietness. I should keep wearing my EMF bracelet. Just at that moment, without my even being there, it fell on the floor of our home, and my father picked it up and put it back on the table. Then he saw after some time that it had fallen onto the floor again in the same spot he picked it up before. When I came home and sat down on the sofa, I saw my bracelet on the table, so I put it on, and immediately my hacking stopped. I felt at ease. After a whole day of coughing, my lungs were finally at rest. After I put it on, my father told me what had happened. He said, "It was a very strange experience. I was the only one in the room at the time. It could not have just fallen onto the floor like that." He told me that after I put it on. So, no, it wasn't my psyche playing tricks on me about the bracelet healing my coughing.

Sometimes we just have to believe and accept things that don't make sense to us. Like I always say, objects are energy, and when you see them as that, they will work with you. I told my father not to worry. I explained that what he experienced was my accumulated energy that I'd put into this EMF bracelet. Now it's back on my wrist, keeping me healthy again.

I wear my pyrite rock, too. I wear it close to my chest. I always ask the pyrite, "Hey, keep my lungs healthy today." I was told by Gods to press the pyrite into my chest, like working with an acupressure point. I did that, and yes, that keeps my lungs in check, too. You have to speak to the rocks and stones for healing. You have to see and feel their energy and let them do what they're meant to do for you.

There are no objects in my life. There is only an abundance of dancing energy. I see it and feel it. I am part of it, just as it is part of me. We are one. I speak to the ocean, and it says to me: "I am here to heal you. You must stay near me." I respond: "I'm coming." Even when I'm not near the ocean at that moment, I still speak to it. We speak a language without words and dialogue, and we hear it. I call the ocean by its name, and it heals me from a distance.

I couldn't believe it. Tonight was the big night. I was ready: "Bring it on – I can handle it!" I had cousins visiting from NYC. Whenever the family gets together, it's always one big party. We have a great time, and there's a lot of unspoken love between all of us. We were going to a nightclub, and I thought to myself, "How am I gonna survive this?" Loud music, screaming voices, lungs shot from yelling all night just to get in a conversation. Oh, my God! But I was prepared. I had my stones on. I had one in my bra, one around my neck, and my EMF bracelet on my wrist. My cousins ordered bottle service, so we know what that means. Big money, big partying. I had fifteen smokers all around me. Yes, they could smoke, because the club was on the rooftop. I thought, "Okay, stones, do your thing – help me out!" And they did. I couldn't believe it. Fifteen smoking drunks inches away from me all night, and my lungs survived. I was even okay the next day. Sure, I had some irritable coughing, but I wasn't KO'd. There was a time when I couldn't even be around one smoker, and that night there were more than my ten little fingers could count. This went on all night – cigarettes, cigars, joints.

Now, I'm not going to make a habit of being around smoke all the time. That would be asking for trouble. But I got my validation. Divine nature in the form of gemstones was my saviour. Hats off to my crystals and rocks. I have a whole new level of respect for them now. Gems have healing properties, but you must open your heart to them. Let them give you the protection they're meant to give. Love your stones. Speak to them, ask of them what you want, and watch them deliver. I feel at one with the stones. I feel what they feel. I hear what they say. Our energies are in sync.

My first experience with appreciating stones was with my sunset topaz that I wore many years back. At that time I wasn't even involved in any kind of heightened consciousness practice. I was a lost soul back then. But the stone still gave me its energy, perhaps because I was open to receiving it. We became one. Everything you touch and everything you think is a real energy that responds to you. If you see yourself as continuous energy, and if the things around you are of the same energy, there will be an easy exchange of giving and receiving. Today I hit the arm of a wooden chair by accident with my computer. It was a pretty hard hit – my metal Apple laptop hitting the wooden chair, which is soft and gentle. I felt compassion for the chair I'd banged, and I apologized. "Ooh, I'm sorry!" Then I caressed the part that I'd hit and gave it love. The chair's energy gave me love back, and I received it.

You might have a hard time imagining that a spiritual being who leads a pretty quiet lifestyle could also end up at an intimate gathering in a posh penthouse suite overlooking the skyline – a breath-taking panoramic view of city skyscrapers. Definitely a millionaire's palace. Yes, I was there taking part. How wonderful! I say "wonderful" because you learn something new every day. That day I learnt a lot about things I'd ever known before.

They all knew I was a spiritual mentor and healer. Maybe that was the reason I was accepted there. I myself don't pass judgement on anyone. I'm happy to just be a part of whatever circles want to accept me as I accept them. That puts us in a position where we can all learn from each other, no matter what the topic. Our hearts are open to gathering information and expanding love to those who need it. I think it's good to have a variety of people at small gatherings, since everyone can contribute somehow. The conversation flowed smoothly. They spoke about what they knew, and I spoke about what I knew. They were intrigued to hear about my spiritual info, and I was thrilled to listen to their topics of choice.

This intimate gathering got my channelling energies flowing. And what I picked up on was that everybody needs love. Why do people gather together, anyhow? To have fun, share their interests and maybe learn new things. The people there were different from me, but it didn't matter. Everybody was looking for what they had in common, which was sharing and comfortableness – and that's a form of love. It's about connecting with other human beings, souls that are maybe very different from you and have different views from your own. But if you can come together and share, knowing that there's no judgement, then that's love. That's what my experience was with these people. I felt very connected to them. I think there was a lot of love in the room.

I started wondering how I could help them see what I see. How could I bring spirituality into their lives in a way that they could see it as stimulating and intriguing? Not the boring cliché picture of people sitting there for hours on end until they see a white light. No, that wouldn't fly with this group. They live for excitement and risk – they're the types that like to live on the edge.

I'm still thinking about it. I think my personally augmented style of kundalini tantra would suit them. I'm sure just hearing about tantra would at least pique their interest. But spreading love is really the best and most rewarding thing you can do. I want to spread my love amongst new circles of friends anytime and all the time. I know there are many more people like them out there. This was just a small fraction … and it was a privilege to interact with them intimately.

What a wonderful way to spend Canada Day! I went to the Amma Canada event. I wanted to be amongst the 32 million people who have received her hugs. To see and be in the presence of such a vibrant soul is an honour. Amma did not stop hugging for over twelve hours straight – no breaks. That by itself sends out high vibrations and elevates others by giving them of her inner stamina and strength. At no time did I see the smile drop from her graceful face. There was no shortage of light to anyone. She is no doubt a divine energy. She has the blessing of all the Divine Lights bestowed upon her. She keeps hugging and smiling and not dimming at all.

It was a very new experience for me, as I have never seen a woman spiritual leader speak before. I have gravitated more towards male spiritual leaders. That's just the way it has gone for me. I never even thought much about the existence of women spiritual leaders. But they do exist, although there are far more men who are spiritual leaders out there than women, so I'm glad I got to experience the light of a female spiritual soul.

I bought a coconut as darshan for Amma and got in line with the hundreds of others in front of me. My heart started beating fast as I got closer. But then a calmness came over me the closer I got to her. At that moment, I realized I was ready. I was ready for the world. I was ready for the duties and the special role that I, too, was meant to serve on this planet. In all my past meetings with saints and gurus, I always got quite emotional. Not this time. It was wonderful to witness it. I was only a few people away from receiving my Amma hug. When it came my turn, I got my hug and blessings from Amma. She gave me a sweet little kiss as prashad – a Hershey's kiss. Some people were getting malas and flowers thrown on them as prashad. I was completely content with my Hershey's kiss. Others perhaps needed the malas and flowers more than I did. But all of us received exactly what made sense for us at that time in our lives. A Hershey's kiss, a mala, a flower – they're all beautiful prashads to embrace and accept, especially since they're given with pure love and intention.

BEING AMY

We can all be AMY

You have to be spiritual. You have to think spiritually because you are a spiritual being – nothing more. Your body is temporary, so don't be too attached to it. Live this outward life, and live it well. Be a part of the game. Play hard, work hard, create meaning and purpose, and leave a good imprint behind.

Embrace all things that come your way, even the things you don't like. Embrace yourself. Everything is beauty, including you. Love yourself – your spiritual self. Then it will be easy to love and understand others. Don't think too hard. Just be. Just do.

I have an old friend from my younger days, when I was twelve years old. We're still friends today. She is a blue-eyed, blonde white girl who is probably more Indian than I am. She sent me a beautiful message on Diwali in 2012. On 13 November, she sent a text, first of all wishing me a Joyous Diwali. Diwali is the celebration of the god Ram, who comes back to the city after being in exile for fourteen years. He was a lot like Krishna and Jesus, spending much of his time in the forest and the open wilderness, and for fourteen years he met with sages and saints and preached the higher life. Diwali is the celebration in Indian culture of when Ram finally comes back home after so many years, and the festival is celebrated by lighting many candles. All the lights in the houses stay on that day, and candles are lit outside on the front doorsteps to bless the homes and all that enter into them. The spiritual meaning behind it is to always have bright lights and growth and prosperity in our lives – to come out of the darkness and celebrate life, to rejoice in it.

My childhood friend sent me not only Diwali wishes that day but another loving message that said, "Oh, there are lights everywhere! You really inspire me, sister! Continue to spread it, speak it and be it. Much love and adoration." I was taken away by her kind and encouraging words. I knew she spoke from her heart. I told her, "I will do this. I will hold your words close to me. These words give me encouragement."

Listen … we can all be AMY – A Modern Yogi.

179

GLOSSARY

Ajna chakra – the sixth chakra, or Third Eye chakra

Asanas – yogic exercises, or postures

Ayahuasca – a psychoactive Amazonian plant-based drink used in healing and shamanic initiatory practices

Chakra – one of the seven major yogic psychic centers relating to different aspects of the human being. Starting from the base of the spine and proceeding to the top of the head, they are: the root, sacral, solar plexus, heart, throat, brow (or Third Eye), and crown chakra.

Darshan – a devotional gift; a blessing or bestowal of love, light and grace

EMF – electromagnetic field

Ganesha – Hindu elephant god

Hat Yog – Hatha Yoga; the form of yoga that is mostly concerned with physical exercises

Malas – prayer beads

Mata Vaishnu – Also Mata Vaishno Devi; a holy temple in the northern Indian town of Katra in Himachal Pradesh

Murti – the image of a deity

Nadis – Kundalini channels

Prana – the subtle life force in all things. It is most directly accessed through the breath, but it is a subtler substance than air.

Prashad – in this case, a blessing; also, an offering or gift

Red serpent – symbol of kundalini awakening

Sadhu – yogi renunciate or ascetic

Shakti – cosmic or spiritual energy; the creative power of the Divine Feminine

Shiv Lok (also, Shiva Loka) – Dev Lok, which is before Shiv Lok, is the angelic realm. Shiv Lok is above the angelic realm. Shiv Lok is the higher astral realms.

Siddhi – super- or paranormal powers; spiritual power

Sukhasan – easy sitting pose in yoga

Thali – an Indian meal made up of a selection of various dishes, often used as a form darshan (a devotional gift)

Tratak – one-pointed concentration on an external object

ABOUT THE AUTHOR

Charu Puri is a healer, spiritual mentor, writer and modern-day yogi. Trained in India, she has spent a decade helping people from around the world to find their path towards self-knowledge.

Come awaken your self-knowledge and ignite your inner fire!

Visit me at
www.amodernyogi.com
and
youtube.com- A Modern Yogi

www.ingramcontent.com/pod-product-compliance
Lightning Source LLC
Chambersburg PA
CBHW060442040426
42331CB00043B/1003